W9-DEO-507

THE DEVELOPMENT OF
HIGHER EDUCATION
IN MEXICO

THE DEVELOPMENT OF HIGHER EDUCATION IN MEXICO

By George I. Sánchez

PROFESSOR OF
LATIN AMERICAN EDUCATION
THE UNIVERSITY OF TEXAS

GREENWOOD PRESS, PUBLISHERS
WESTPORT, CONNECTICUT

LA
427
.S3
1970

INTRODUCTION

THE oldest university town in North America and the most beautiful is Morelia. It lies in the heart of the Mexican uplands at the opening of what might be called the lake country of Mexico. After long miles of driving over mountain roads one descends into a lush valley alongside of an aqueduct whose lofty arches of solid masonry bear the impress of Spanish engineers who kept alive the traditions of ancient Rome. The lofty and massive cathedral and the public square beside it, with its shadowy arcades, seem lifted bodily from the Spain of the late Middle Ages. It is a fitting home for an institution of learning which can claim with some justification the longest continuous history of any such institution in the new world. For it is the continuation of the college founded at Patzquaro in 1540, only twenty years after the Conquest by Cortés, for the religious education of both Indians and Spaniards, and later moved to its present site to the town then called Valladolid which was later to bear the name Morelia in honor of one of its greatest citizens, the patriot, Morelos. This is not the place to recall its checkered history, for that is given in the pages which follow, but there could be no better introduction to the whole theme of this volume than by way of the University of Morelia which has from time to time refreshed not only the intellectual life of Mexico, but also its political and social history. It is a narrative rich with the lessons of human experience. For the school, founded for the study of theology and religion, became a center of nationalism and of radical reform, in short, a real mirror of the history of Mexico.

There is an added advantage in starting with the history of education in a provincial town because the history of higher education in Mexico City itself is more complex and therefore, to the foreign observer, somewhat confusing. Indeed, this is the impression made by the Mexican educational system upon those foreign observers who have failed to be acclimated to the unique social and economic problems of Mexico.

Looking only at externals, it might seem as though higher education in Mexico had not been integrated into the changing social and political life

of the country as definitely as has been the case elsewhere, and more
especially in the United States. But as we have just indicated, and as this
study clearly shows, this impression of conservative educational methods,
predominantly Spanish or clerical, is by no means borne out by the facts.
While it is true that up until recently the equipment for scientific education in Mexico has not kept pace with the needs of the situation, and the
methods of instruction differ from those in vogue in the United States,
no one can deny the existence of keen intellectual interest in all the
problems of today.

In the illuminating study which follows, Professor George I. Sánchez
has traced both the historical background and the situation in Mexican
higher education today, viewing both subjects with a sympathetic and
impartial eye. Wherever critical comments occur they do not differ in
either kind or degree from those which any discerning educational expert
is bound to make concerning our own system of education. The degree
of achievement in all such matters depends upon the means which are
available fully as much as upon enlightened leadership. The fact that
the natural wealth of Mexico is chiefly concentrated in a few industries,
and that many of the agricultural workers of the native population live
close to the limits of subsistence, must be kept in mind in judging the
progress which has been made in recent years. It is but right, therefore,
that the chief interest has been in the development of primary and
secondary education rather than of the university work at the higher
level. Upon the whole, however, there is notable achievement in spite
of setbacks, and in this discriminating but friendly narrative we have an
authoritative account of serious and high-minded efforts to maintain
higher education in Mexico on a level consonant with the keen intellectual
capacity of the people concerned. Dr. Sánchez has had unusual facilities
for getting to the heart of the problems involved and his volume is a
valuable contribution in the field of international intellectual cooperation.

JAMES T. SHOTWELL

CONTENTS

Chapter One

THE CULTURAL SCENE

INTRODUCTION

THE DEVELOPMENT of education in Mexico offers a confusing array of
seemingly contradictory trends and events. The Mexican educational
scene is a panorama of liberal principles and reactionary practice, of achievement and failure, of creativeness and mimicry. A casual perusal of that
nation's history of education leaves the student bewildered at what appears
to be an astonishing lack of consistency and continuity in policies and
programs. At first glance there appears to be neither a well-defined pattern
of development nor an understandable reason for its absence. It would
seem that, in education, Mexico has proceeded on a trial and error basis
and that it has never hit upon a scheme of ideas or a plan of action that
has satisfied it for long. Thus one might well be led to believe that Mexican
culture has not achieved an educational point of view, and that it has not
yet given rise to criteria which are valid in the evaluation of its own processes or adequate for more than a brief span of the nation's history.

Mexico presents a picture of accomplishments and deficiencies, of readily
apparent inconsistencies and conflicts between theory and practice. This is
particularly true for those students of education in the United States, who,
guided by events in their own country, seek to assess Mexican education
on the basis of the values, the achievements, and the historical pattern
which obtained in the development of schools in the United States. From
the viewpoint derived from the study of the course which educational
events have taken there, it is easy to arrive at an erroneous evaluation of
the Mexican educational scene, itself. Some of the cultural factors which
influenced education in the United States were not operative in Mexico.
Other factors, though common to both, were conditioned by circumstances
which differed widely in the two countries; and still other cultural factors
varied in significance in the two settings. These differences and variations
represent distinguishing basic considerations of which due account must
be taken before comparisons of the educational programs are made. Approached from the point of departure offered by the cultural determinants

affecting Mexican education, the confusing panorama referred to above assumes greater coherence and meaning, justifications are more readily discerned, and what otherwise might be regarded as paradoxical or the expression of perverseness becomes understandable. The accomplishments and deficiencies observable at first glance attain a new meaning and become elements which fit into tendencies and trends. These, in turn, studied in the light of their causes and effects, serve not only as the basis for judging the past but also as criteria for the present and as guideposts or warnings in the matter of future developments.

The development of education in Mexico cannot be thought of apart from the vital currents and issues which contributed to the evolution of a Mexican society. It would be a serious mistake to seek to describe the history of Mexican education without regard for the cultural factors and movements which constitute the Mexican heritage. In the final analysis, educational aims and procedures are merely products of larger social motives and conditions; for educational processes and institutions, their ways and their ends, stem from national or racial culture. A true evaluation of those institutions cannot be made except in so much as one's judgment takes due account of time and place, the human elements involved, and the schemes of values operating in the social phenomena concerned.

These broad considerations are of particular significance in the study of Mexican education. While Mexican schools spring from European origins, it should not be overlooked that the European patterns were not simply translated to a docile and virgin setting. Mexico was not a wilderness or a cultural vacuum. The process of transplanting European civilization to New Spain involved the inter-action of cultures, the realignment of policies, the adjustment of schemes of values, and the process uprooted the indigenous cultures. That is common knowledge. What is often overlooked is that the process also involved a fundamental reorienting of the European pattern. It changed the Indian but not without altering the Spaniard.

The reciprocal effects of culture contacts are inevitable. Furthermore, the contact between the European and the Indian produced among Indians and Spaniards something more than merely new views and new ways of doing things. It produced a new people. The *mestizo* is an important factor in the development of Mexican culture.

It would take more time and space than is at present available to dwell at length upon the implications of these considerations. Their effect upon

Mexican cultural growth and development is evidenced in many subtle ways requiring a more comprehensive analysis than can be given here. Only the salient effects will be referred to, from time to time, in the course of this study. The following sections summarize the major considerations which have influenced the nature and course of education in Mexico.

THE GEOGRAPHICAL FACTOR

A common source of error in appraising the Mexican scene arises from inadequate knowledge of its geography. This is particularly true when we consider the part that Mexico's natural resources have played in the evolution of its institutions and its schemes of value. As Sánchez Mejorada says in his article on communications and transportation in Mexico,[1]

The shape and topography of the country, its location and relation to the other countries of the world, the products of its soil, both those which serve as sustenance to its inhabitants and those which it exchanges for the products of other nations, the distribution and density of its population, determine and explain the development of its means of communication.

He might have said, with equal truth, that those same factors weigh heavily in determining and explaining both cultural development as a whole, and —of special import to us here—the development of education. One cannot think of the nature and scope of education without thinking of the means of communication used among the peoples involved and of the material resources upon which the entire social structure rests.

Topography and terrain alone are important elements which determine or, at least, condition cultural growth. Gamio suggests this when he speaks of Mexico's "adverse terrain." [2]

The geographical factor which has proved a fundamental obstacle to social development and from which are derived the other factors that have affected it adversely, consists in the very rough and highly diversified character of the Mexican terrain. Mountains, cliffs, and gorges— that is to say, rugged land—constitute probably more than half the total area of the country, and in these regions farming and even the exploita-

[1] Javier Sánchez Mejorada, *Mexico Today, Annals of the American Academy of Political and Social Science,* March, 1940, Vol. 208, p. 78.

[2] Manuel Gamio, *Mexico Today,* "Geographic and Social Handicaps," *Annals of the American Academy of Political and Social Science,* March, 1940, Vol. 208, p. 4.

tion of raw materials is very difficult if not impossible. This topography has made it difficult to communicate and to carry on commercial and other kinds of interchange between the several regions of Mexico, many of which still remain in the same isolated situation in which they were centuries ago. The railroads and highways built in the last seventy-five years have improved the situation somewhat, but it has been impossible to provide all that were needed, because the cost of construction in such rugged terrain is very great in view of the limitations of the national budget. The disadvantages described above would have been compensated if the upheavals of remote geological epochs had raised the peaks of the mountains and volcanoes to a still greater elevation, for in that case many of them would be sufficiently covered with perpetual snow to form high, plentiful, and constant sources of irrigation; whereas actually these occur only on the Pico de Orizaba, Popocatépetl, and Iztaccíhuatl.

These differences in altitude, combined with differences in latitude, temperature, hydrography, rainfall, and geological, mineralogical, and other factors, have helped to form many distinct climatic regions, different types of plant and animal life, and different biological characteristics in the inhabitants, especially in the Indians who have lived for thousands of years in this multiform environment.

As Gamio points out in the study referred to, these elements have proven less favorable to human development in Mexico than in such other American nations as Argentina and the United States. This is made clear by comparing population growth. During the last 160 years, the population of Mexico has increased in the ratio of 3 to 1, that of the United States 14 to 1, and Argentina's, 25 to 1. During that period Brazil's population has multiplied 16 times. It is, of course, not to be assumed that geography was the sole factor operating in producing these results, but its influence as a contributing factor cannot be disregarded. In Mexico, certainly, geographical limitations played a highly important part in keeping down this ratio. Regardless of the potential values which Mexico's geography may offer for future growth, these potentialities were inoperative in the past. Viewing Mexican achievements in retrospect, with proper regard for the time at which events took place and for the means available to the people of that time, one cannot but see in the nation's physical features powerful deterrents to social development.

It is quite common to hear glowing accounts of Mexico's natural wealth and to find her widely regarded as a vast treasure house. As a consequence, directly or by implication, the Mexican is portrayed as a ragged and indolent creature sitting upon a pot of gold. An objective analysis will quickly give the lie to such a myth. It can even be argued that, though the mineral resources of New Spain have produced large sums, the exploitation of these resources have been heavily subsidized—subsidized by the misery of forced labor and by methods that have been ruthless. The myth has also had a source in an unrealistic appraisal of the nation's mineral wealth. It is true that mineral products make up for some 70 per cent of the value of Mexico's exports, and that in the last five centuries Mexico has produced almost half of the world's total output of silver. These facts have been popularly accepted without critical analysis, and the world has mistakenly come to base its estimates of Mexico's wealth on the gross values represented in the export of her production of oil and metals.

When the mineral wealth of Mexico is appraised against its human background, a less glowing picture comes to light. For example, based on the census of 1930, it is estimated [3] that production by these industries represented about $113,000,000 pesos out of a total national income of slightly more than two billions. This means about six pesos, of a total of some one hundred and twenty pesos for Mexico's per capita income. Even this is qualified by the fact that, until recently, much of this wealth went, not to the people of Mexico, but to foreign companies. Seen from another angle, the mining industry represents about 6 per cent of the total national wealth and amounts to 35 pesos per capita as against a total of 616 pesos. All this makes it plain that mineral production, by which Mexican wealth is often judged, is in reality not only not a representative item but it also does not constitute a source of large returns to the people. These figures also make it evident that the total national income, translated into per capita figures, is very low, or some $35 in Mexico as compared with more than $650 in the United States.

With due regard for the fact that, though they do not assume the proportions commonly assigned to them, the mineral resources constitute an important phase of Mexico's economic life, the real foundation of her economy lies in agriculture. This is brought out clearly in President Avila Camacho's recent address to the Mexican Agronomical Society. On that

[3] Secretaría de la Economiá Nacional, *México En Cifras,* Dirección General de Estadística, 1938.

occasion he stated that, while Mexico must not neglect her industrial development, such development should be planned to complement her agriculture—for Mexico is first of all an agricultural country and agriculture must continue to be her chief concern.[4]

Though there may be a difference of opinion as to the place that agriculture will occupy in the future with relation to other phases of the national economy, there is no denying the fact the Mexican economy is now and has always been an essentially agrarian economy. It may be that, by suitable and complementary industries and through improved methods of exploitation, this economic base can be made more fruitful. It is also possible that such reforms, coupled with a changed international situation in Mexico may assume a more favorable economic part than has been the case in the past, and result in a more abundant life for Mexicans. However, all that remains for future determination. Obviously, these possibilities, no matter how probable, do not enter into an evaluation of the role that the economic factor has played in past cultural developments except as, in recent years, they have formed the basis for future planning. It is the consensus of all competent observers that, insofar as the past is concerned, Mexico's wealth has been in agriculture and that her agrarian economy has been an impoverished one. The views of Chester Lloyd Jones in this regard are typical.[5]

All in all, a first survey of Mexico indicates it to be a country of limited and specialized agricultural resources which have been only partly brought into yield by a population not yet in full touch with modern methods. Advance in foodstuff production is still possible, but there are no great areas which await development. Though the Republic has an area about equal to 85 per cent of the land of the United States east of the Mississippi River, its corn crop, the greatest reliance for food for man and animals, is less than a sixth of the average crop of Iowa. Wheat and beans are next in yield, but the wheat yield is about one-fifteenth of that of Kansas, and the bean crop one-twelfth of that of Michigan.

This means that the development of social institutions has been founded upon inadequacy and poverty.

[4] Manuel Avila Camacho, "México Debe Ser País Agricola E Industrial," Secretaría de Gobernación, Mexico, 1941.

[5] Chester Lloyd Jones, "Production of Wealth in Mexico," Mexico Today, Annals of the American Academy of Political and Social Science, March, 1940, Vol. 208, p. 56.

It takes no elaborate analysis to demonstrate Mexico's agricultural poverty. Her agricultural area totals less than fifteen million hectares, only eleven per cent of the area of the nation. This represents less than one hectare per capita. Of this area, less than 60 per cent is under cultivation and, of that, only about 80 per cent is harvested.[6] This means that there is less than half a hectare of productive land per capita. Add to this the fact that the productivity of much of it is seriously limited by such factors as inadequate water supply and poor soil conditions, and it will be evident that, though agriculture is Mexico's primary economic base, Mexican agriculture does not constitute the foundation for an abundant economy. Even after years of intensive attack, the report of the Cárdenas administration makes clear the marked poverty of Mexican agriculture.[7]

"Mexico is not a rich country, but an extremely poor one." So says Federico Bach, Mexican economist, in his article on "The Distribution of Wealth in Mexico." [8] Elsewhere (p. 73) in that study he has this to say:

In regard to agriculture as well as minerals, Mexico is extremely poor for natural reasons, and will not produce enough to feed its people until there has been an expensive intensification of farming and an enormous investment of capital to solve the greatest problem of all—the water supply. While Nature was kind to Mexico in regard to the great variety of climate, it was not so in regard to water. Nearly the entire country suffers periodically from scarcity of water, and since Mexico does not have important rivers, irrigation systems can be provided only by means of a large outlay of capital, the individual farmer could probably never make singlehanded.

Agriculture has never been an important source of income in Mexico, either in the colonial period or subsequently, although the majority of the population lives by it. If the population employed in agriculture had enjoyed a proper standard of living, production would always have been insufficient. Just as mining enterprises were self-supporting only because the mine workers received starvation wages, so the cultivation of enormous landed estates was possible only because the peons were in a state of virtual slavery.

[6] See *México En Cifras*, 1934, pp. 41–42; and *La Reforma Agraria En México*, 1937, Lámina 10; Secretaría de la Economía Nacional, Dirección General de Estadística.

[7] Secretaría de Gobernación, Departamento de Plan Sexenal. *Seis Años de Gobierno al Servicio de México, 1934–1940.* Mexico, La Nacional Impresora S. A., 1940, pp. 111–154.

[8] Federico Bach, *Mexico Today, Annals of The American Academy of Political and Social Science*, March, 1940, Vol. 208, p. 77.

In this article (p. 70), Bach summarizes his examination of Mexican economy thus:

> A cool and impartial analysis of its economic resources brings us to the conclusion that Mexico, far from deserving its reputation for natural wealth, must be placed among those countries which are by nature poor and in which wealth may be produced only by dint of enormous sacrifices on the part of their people. The investigator becomes aware that although enormous riches have in fact been extracted from the soil of Mexico, they were obtained only because the standard of living of the population was very low. Sweat and hunger have always been the producers of wealth in Mexico.

The geographical factor, then, is seen to loom large in the Mexican cultural scene. As will be observed later, this physical setting, upon which educational events were projected, has done much to determine the nature and course of the history of education. It should be noted here that the effects of geographical limitations are not only such as can be deduced from economic inadequacy for the support of institutions. There are numerous subtle ways in which these limitations make themselves felt—popular attitudes and beliefs, class lines, social values, and the like. Reading between the lines of the history of education in Mexico, the careful student will find many evidences of the determining influence exercised by the factor of geography.

CULTURE CONTACTS AND CONFLICTS

It has been said at the beginning of this chapter that pre-Columbian Mexico was neither a wilderness nor a cultural vacuum. That statement requires no substantiation here as at least the general facts of Indian life in Mexico are of common knowledge. What is sometimes overlooked is that these facts have had important implications for the subsequent evolution of a Mexican nation. It has been estimated that there were at least 10,000,000 Indians in Mexico at the time of the Conquest. On this point Molina Enríquez states: [9]

> We do not believe it would be foolhardly to assert that the more than six hundred (Indian) groups indicated by the facts in the case . . . must have numbered no less than twenty-five million inhabitants. There are

[9] Andrés Molina Enríquez, *La Revolución Agraria De México*. México, Museo Nacional de Arqueología Historia y Etnografía, 1932. Vol. I, 70.

many data to support the approximate truth of that figure; but we may reduce it to fifteen or ten million.

While the figure of 10,000,000 is probably an exaggeration, the fact that there were at least two million or more Indians in early New Spain is highly significant in the explanation of population growth, of land use and management, and of educational policies. The added fact that these people spoke many different tongues, that they were dispersed over a wide extent of territory, and that they were grouped into what, in effect, were separate nations, are not to be taken lightly in the evaluation of the results which attended the establishment of European institutions. Moreover, the nature and direction of indigenous cultural attainments warrant careful study in any attempt to judge Mexican social attitudes and goals.

Reference to Basauri's ethnographic presentation of the indigenous population of Mexico shows that the significance of Indian life in Mexico goes beyond biological considerations or statistical portrayal.[10] The accompanying table offers evidence of the linguistic complexity that is evident in the indigenous scene even today. These data are well illustrated and elaborated further in the volume *Seis Años De Gobierno Al Servicio De México*.[11] Yet even these figures do not reveal the situation in all its impressive significance. This is suggested by Redfield in his excellent summary of "The Indian In Mexico" where he writes: [12]

The "fifty-four" different languages in terms of which the census enumerates the Indian-speaking population are not to be taken as a definite and exhaustive list. Some language-names listed are known by linguists to include several notably different languages, while others listed separately are hardly dialectic variants of one another. The fact of consequence is the great linguistic diversity, with the cultural separateness that accompanies it. In southern Mexico there are local markets where Indians meet who speak languages as different from one another as are English, Chinese, and Hebrew. Although there are great differences in this respect, on the whole in southern Mexico the Indians have tended to marry within their own ethnic groups. One reflection of this fact is that although conforming to the same general physical type, there are

[10] Carlos Basauri, *La Población Indígena De México*. Mexico, Secretaría de Educación Pública, Oficina Editora Popular, 1940. Volumes I, II.

[11] Secretaría de Gobernación, *op. cit.*, pp. 351–382.

[12] Robert Redfield, *Mexico Today, The Annals of the American Academy of Political and Social Science*, March, 1940, Vol. 208, p. 135.

LINGUISTIC FAMILIES*

With subdivisions by Dialects

	Total Speaking Language or Dialect	Total in Linguistic Family
YUMANOS		125
a).—Cucapas	14	
b).—Kilihuis	80	
c).—Huaipais	31	
SERIANA		160
a).—Kunkaks o seris	160	
PIMANA		68,210
a).—Papagos	535	
b).—Opatas	40	
c).—Pimas	860	
d).—Yaquis	7,183	
e).—Mayos	26,815	
f).—Ocoronis	85	
g).—Tarahumaras	26,834	
h).—Guarigias (Varogios)	1,120	
i).—Tepehuanes	4,738	
NAHUATLANA		685,389
a).—Coras	2,365	
b).—Huicholes	3,716	
c).—Tepecanos (Tepehuan Mexicano) ...	99	
d).—Mexicanos (Nahoas)	670,595	
e).—Cuitlatecos	118	
f).—Chontales de Oaxaca	8,496	
TARASCANA		44,371
a).—Tarascos	44,371	
ALGONQUINIANA		495
a).—Kikapoos	495	
ATAPASCANA		451
a).—Chichimecas jonaces	451	
OTOMIANA		299,291
a).—Otomies	218,811	
b).—Mazahuas	77,715	
c).—Chichimecas pames	2,765	

	Total Speaking Language or Dialect	Total in Linguistic Family
MATLATZINCANA	1,167	1,167
MIXTECO-ZAPOTECANA		501,131
a).—Mixtecos	172,114	
b).—Zapotecas	216,825	
c).—Amuzgos	8,247	
d).—Triques	2,741	
e).—Chatinos	11,739	
f).—Mazatecos	55,343	
g).—Cuicatecos	9,221	
h).—Chinantecos	24,073	
i).—Ojitecos	172	
j).—Ixcatecos	656	
TOTONACANA		94,211
a).—Totonacos	90,425	
b).—Tepehuas	3,786	
ZOQUE-MIXEANA		96,607
a).—Zoques	20,969	
b).—Mixes	31,698	
c).—Yavanas	91	
d).—Tlapanecos	16,479	
e).—Chochos	2,308	
f).—Popolocas	20,927	
g).—Huaves	4,135	
MAYA-QUICHEANA		457,628
a).—Huaxtecos	41,271	
b).—Chontal de Tabasco	15,610	
c).—Mayas	279,093	
d).—Choles	16,903	
e).—Tzotziles	34,253	
f).—Zeltales	40,342	
g).—Tojolabales	8,471	
h).—Mames	21,685	
i).—Lacandones (Approximately 200. This figure not to be added to others.)		
NOT CLASSIFIED	160	160
TOTAL	2,249,396	2,249,396

* Adapted from *México En Cifras*, Secretaría de La Economía Nacional, 1934. p. 14.

great differences as between tribes, while there is homogeneity within each isolated group. Mexico includes some of the tallest Indians known, and some of the shortest. Starr found the Tzendal to be a long-headed people, while the Yucatec Maya, linguistically related, are very broad-headed (cephalic index of 77 as compared with 85).

The facts alluded to above refer largely to the conditions prevalent today when the process of acculturation, within the indigenous groups and between Indians and Europeans, has had the advantage of several centuries of development. These conditions, projected back to the period when the nation was acquiring its dominant cultural characteristics and when it was laying the foundations of its civilization, were not only more extensive and more complex but their effects upon culture contacts were much more striking. The language problem, alone, constituted a serious determinant in the inter-cultural adjustments which were called for when Europeans came into contact with the Indian peoples. Basauri says: [13]

The first cultural shock between Europeans and the population of America was, without doubt, occasioned by language difference. This difference established a barrier that for a long time was almost impenetrable and the intellectual contact between conquerors and conquered was carried on very slowly along two avenues: one, the learning of indigenous tongues by the Spaniards, principally by the missionaries, and, the other, the acquisition of the Spanish tongue by the Indians. In the first years of the Colony the number of Spaniards who learned aboriginal languages was relatively larger than the number of Indians who could express themselves in Spanish. The procedure for the purposes of catechisation and for those of the Spanish throne could not achieve better results. The Indians did not lack self confidence. They were receptive to those who spoke to them in their own language. But the inculcation of the Catholic religion was effected only through a system of translating the theology and dogma of Christianity into the indigenous tongues.

Moreover, while the missionaries spoke to the Indian in his own idiom, an official language was also established, the Spanish that was the language of the oppressors. For the *encomenderos,* the *patrones,* the official authorities, etc., used it, and therefore, for the Indians, everyone who spoke Spanish was their hierarchical superior or their exploiter.

[13] Basauri, *op. cit.,* pp. 116–117.

The psychological implications arising out of the language problem which are suggested by Basauri bear close scrutiny when we seek to appraise the Indian's influence upon cultural development. Their importance is suggested by recent investigations dealing with analogous situations elsewhere in the world. In reviewing studies made of various language groups, the present writer has said this: [14]

These studies indicate that a foreign home-language is a serious handicap which involves not only an inability to use with efficiency the school language but in some instances it has been suggested also that bilingualism is responsible for a mental confusion which hinders the expression of possible innate ability.

The language barrier, as an obstacle to social intercourse alone, is a factor which weighs heavily in the functioning of any society. When the additional barriers of a caste system are superimposed on the already staggering handicap arising out of the language differences confronting a people, the magnitude of the obstacles to acculturation becomes overwhelming. This is especially true when it is realized that, in addition, the contact in Mexico was between Spanish and a wide variety of non-European languages. The psychological effects which this situation had upon both Indians and Spaniards were of no small consequence in determining both the kind of programs which were established to govern their relationships but also the rate and the direction of growth of those programs.

The language differences and the problems arising therefrom simply symbolize the much larger questions comprised in cultural differences. Mexico's Indian peoples had their social institutions, their systems of values, their techniques. Through past centuries they had been responding to the geographical factor, to culture contacts and conflicts. Each tribe or "nation" had evolved its own way of life, its personality. These cultural personalities showed individual differences between nation and nation—in language, in forms of governments, in ethical values. They also differed in the number and development of the tools of civilization. For example, Mayan chronology was highly complex and abstract.[15] The civilization of the Tarahumaras, on the other hand, did not involve such elaborate tools of

---

[14] George I. Sánchez, "Group Differences and Spanish-Speaking Children—A Critical Review." *Journal of Applied Psychology*, October, 1932, Vol. XVI, No. 5, p. 550.

[15] Juan Enrique Palacios, "El Calendario y Jeroglíficos Cronográficos Mayas," *Primer Centenario de la Sociedad Mexicana de Geografía y Estadística*, Mexico, 1933. Vol. II, 457–635.

this nature.[16] The religious differences were no less pronounced as has been pointed out even by Mendizábal, who advances the view that there existed a fundamental sameness in aboriginal religions.[17]

A study of these cultural differences does more than suggest the enormity of the problems confronting New Spain. It also makes it evident that the indigenous peoples of the area had values which can be regarded as forming important resources for the development of a Mexican culture. Through such a study it becomes clear that the Indian had something to contribute, and that European culture was not the only one involved in the Mexican scene. This means, further, that Mexican life and institutions today must be interpreted not simply as outgrowths of European contributions but also in terms of the native elements which have influenced their development. Certainly, in evaluating social achievements, the criteria of judgment must arise out of an examination of the potentialities inherent in the society. The worth of institutional attainments is measured, in part at least, by the manner and degree to which institutions have responded to the values which surround them. In the case of Mexico, these values—in law and order, in ethical and spiritual concepts, in relationships to property, etc.—stemmed from both European and non-European peoples, and there we find an important consideration in judging social developments. The significance of that consideration is illustrated by Mendizábal.[18] He implies that, while among European peoples punishments are meted out to the lowly while the privileged are immune (or, at best, legal sanctions are the same for all), the Aztecs made the punishment fit not the crime but the rank of the offender—the higher the rank, the greater the punishment!

It is probable that, had the Spaniards come in large numbers to New Spain, the consequences of cultural differences would have been less severe insofar as the implantation of European patterns and tools is concerned. In that case, and at the very worst, it is quite likely that Mexico would today exhibit a cross between the social dualism evidenced in the white-Negro situation in the United States and the Hispano-Americanism of such countries as Argentina and Uruguay. But the Spaniards were few in number, at all times in a ratio of less than one to four. The small number of Spaniards is explained in a variety of ways. Without question such fac-

[16] Basauri, *op. cit.,* Vol. I, 299–352.
[17] Miguel O. de Mendizábal, *Ensayos Sobre Las Civilizaciones Aborígines Americanas.* Mexico, Museo Nacional, 1924, I, 347.
[18] Mendizábal, *ibid.,* p. 125.

tors as Spanish colonial policy and Spain's internal and international situation weighed heavily in limiting the number of colonists. Explanations
based on those factors have often been offered. What is usually disregarded
is that Mexico offered little possibility for widespread colonization.

Large-scale migration from Spain would have entailed far greater resources in New Spain than those which were available. The mining industry
did not call for, nor could it support, great numbers of Europeans. So, too,
with cattle raising. The agricultural resources were not only not highly
attractive but they were largely preëmpted by a native population. Other
economic opportunities were even less appealing. All in all, there was
not much in New Spain that constituted an inducement to heavy immigra-
tion, particularly since, in Spain, conditions were not such that large sections of the population could be deeply motivated in seeking new horizons.
All these elements served to limit cultural contacts and conflicts to a small
number of Europeans on the one hand and to a large number of Indians
on the other.

This disproportion in the racial situation had its consequences in race
relations. The dominant culture was represented by a numerical minority.
Economic resources were limited. The Spaniard could enhance his economic
condition only by encroaching upon the holdings of the majority group or
by exploiting new resources with the labor of its members. In either case,
the Indian was the loser and he was perforce relegated to a socially and
economically inferior position. This process became progressively more
pronounced as, first, the wealth accumulated by the Indians over the
centuries was exhausted and, second, as the number of Europeans and
new institutions increased. This meant, on the one hand, that the possibilities of the Indian to contribute from his culture were growing increasingly
worse, and, on the other, that the dominant group tended to become less
and less responsive to the needs and values represented by the Indian
peoples.

This trend was clearly reflected in subsequent events in both social and
economic spheres. The exploitations of Mexico's natural resources involved
the exploitation of the Indian. Considering the nature and extent of such
resources, the time and place of the events, and the numbers in, and the
social distance between, the dominant and subordinate populations no
other course was feasible. Thus was created Mexico's basic issue, the
struggle among its peoples for the essentials of a livelihood—the agrarian
problem. Jesús Romero Flores, in his annals of the Mexican Revolution,

suggests this as the fundamental cause of his country's social unrest.[19]

Without perverting the interpretation of the facts which make up the history of the Mexican people, and making a calm and impartial study of them (the facts), we will always come to the conclusion that the determining phenomena of the most marked upheavals which have agitated our country have had the economic struggle as their origin. . . . This factor forms the vertebra of our various historical stages.

The first effects of this economic struggle were felt soon after the Conquest when the resources of the area were called upon to support the new burdens introduced with the coming of the conquerors. It is to be noted again, that these new burdens were placed not upon a people or a region with a production surplus but upon an economy that was already heavily taxed to carry the existing load. If, as pointed out before, today there is less than half a hectare of productive land per capita this amount could not have been much more than doubled in the sixteenth century considering the limiting effects of poor systems of communication, of exploitation, etc., of that period. One hectare of land per capita does not constitute the basis for mass well-being. This is particularly true when a sizeable portion of the productive capacity of that land must go to the support of government, church, private profit, and other overhead. In other words, the agrarian problem, already of notable proportions in pre-Columbian days, became a critical issue upon the arrival of new peoples and new institutions.

This issue was no small factor in bringing about the submergence of the Indian, with all which that implies in loss of cultural values. In consequence, as will be noted later, the highly liberal Indian policy of the first stages of the colony rapidly became a dead letter. By the same token, as the economic pressure became greater, social rehabilitation became a matter of decreasing concern in New Spain. Thus, as will be observed when the history of education is examined, the liberal principles upon which educational institutions were founded become less and less reflected in actual practice. The social goals of education become either empty phrases, are confused in practice with unrealistic sophistication, or are so reduced in scope that they are expressed in a narrow and purely academic humanism.

[19] Jesús Romero Flores, *Anales Históricos De La Revolución Mexicana*. Biblioteca Del Maestro. Mexico, El Nacional, 1939. I, 1–2.

The social and economic submergence of the Indian might well have resulted in the virtual obliteration of Indian culture as a contributing factor in the development of Mexico had not two circumstances intervened. As has been mentioned above, the dominant European culture was represented by a relatively small numerical minority of the population. This fact necessitated some adjustments on the part of the Europeans. They had to learn the native languages, they had to depend on native techniques and tools, etc. In this way the subordinate cultures insinuated themselves into that of the governing group. Even so, and judging by analogous situations elsewhere in the world, this process of adjustments and cultural interchange would not have assumed large proportions had it not been for the *mestizo*—the casual but highly significant biological product of racial fusion. Here, indeed, was the human catalyst that was destined to create Mexican nationality. Elsewhere I have summarized the *mestizo* movement thus: [20]

Had the Indian remained in his natural state and had the Spaniard succeeded in his policy of separating the white and bronze races by an unbreakable barrier of class distinction, only the relatively simple problem of articulating subject and governing classes would appear today. However, the circumstances of frontier life and four centuries of close proximity between the two races have made racial mixture and cultural confusion inevitable. Since the earliest days of the Conquest, in spite of antipathies and restrictions, the races have mixed. Indian and Spaniard, *mestizo* and *indio*, Spaniard and *mestizo*, Indian, Spaniards and, to a small degree, Negro have joined to produce a *mestizaje*, a mixture that defies all efforts at definite classification. The *mestizo*, incidental product of two clashing cultures, has arisen slowly to assume the dominant role in Mexico.

The *mestizo*, because he is the by-product of the contact between white and Indian, presents the most complicated picture. Not Indian, yet not European, he is not only a fusion of both but gives evidence of being distinct from either. In a manner of speaking, he alone is Mexican for, contrasted with conquered Indian and conquering Spaniard, he reflects all the elements of the strife and the diverse cultures that make the Mexico of today. Despised and ostracized, reflecting the physical and spiritual strength of the Indian and imbued with the vigour and grace

[20] George I. Sánchez, *Mexico—A Revolution by Education*. (New York, 1936.) pp. 12–15.

of the *conquistador*, he has lifted his head in the midst of negligence and oppression to direct and command the destiny of Mexico. Justo Sierra in his *Manual Escolar de Historia General* has aptly stated:

"The Spaniard despised the Indian infinitely, considering him as a deficient man and as inherently a servant. The *mestizo*, casual product of the dominant and dominated races, he considered capable only of evil, fitted only for theft and homicide. The *mestizo* or half-caste was, nevertheless, the future owner of the country, the future revolutionary, the future author of nationality."

The *mestizo* movement, as the rise of this heterogeneous group may be called for purposes of brevity, permeates all of modern Mexican history. While it has many manifestations and exhibits diverse and often contradictory tendencies, it is essentially a movement for economic and social security—the search of the *mestizos* for a place in the life of the country, a desire to belong. Though the Indian was unfortunate in his servile status and in the loss of the major part of his lands, he possessed a place, mean and distressing as it was, in the order of things. He had kept some of his villages, portions of his ancient communal landholdings, and was part of a homogeneous though subservient culture. He belonged. He could count on the crumbs incident to his exploitation by the superior class and, though he suffered and starved, he was among his kind and was fortified by the pride of race and tradition. The Spaniards, always a small minority of the population, had constituted themselves a superior caste. As a matter of protection and self-preservation, jealous of pre-eminence and privilege, they closed all doors as far as possible against the *mestizos*. The *mestizo* was an unwelcome interloper—he did not belong to either of his parents. While the Spaniard, through a brilliant and courageous conquest, had carved a niche of authority and power for himself, and while the Indian had been relegated to a life of servitude, the *mestizo* could not rule, neither could he serve. He, indeed, was in a limbo of social, political, and economic insecurity. It devolved upon him to nurse the spirit of unrest and rebellion that he might, thereby, make a place for himself in his beloved Mexico.

The Church gave occupation and means of livelihood to many *mestizos*. Many inherited lands from their Spanish fathers and, being closer to the communal pattern of the Indian than to the individualistic character of the Spaniard, soon converted their *haciendas* or tracts into the *ranch-*

erías and *condueñazagos*—the small farms and common ownerships—which still persist. Large numbers returned to a life among the Indians, accentuating an already serious land problem and adding to the spread of a *mestizaje*. Others secured land by means that do not bear close investigation. Still others dedicated themselves to a parasitical roving life or to one of more direct depredation. The problem of an economic location for the *mestizo* arose in early colonial days, contributed largely to the struggles that resulted in independence, started the reform movement of the nineteenth century, found rabid expression in the Revolution of 1910, and is carrying through the agrarian revolution which we witness today.

Even a cursory glance over the pages of Mexican history reveals the profound influence of the *mestizo*. The task of colonial administration was made doubly hard by the socially and economically unattached masses of this culturally irresponsible group. The first hundred years of independence saw *mestizo* leaders and groups striving for emergence from the mire that engulfed them. Lending support first to one movement and then another, their experiences, as *insurgentes* and *revolucionarios* slowly developed a class consciousness and some degree of unanimity of aspirations. The Revolution of 1910 was, basically, a *mestizo* movement, waged by *mestizos* in the interests of a new deal for the underprivileged in Mexico. Beginning as a negligible minority, the *mestizos* now number over eleven million and have become the moving element in Mexican reconstruction. Making common cause with dissatisfied *criollos,* enlisting Indian support, the *mestizo* has symbolized the struggle that has given rise to revolutionary Mexico. Because of the force of numbers and owing to his position of economic insecurity, he has *had* to make his way—socially, politically, and economically. He, of all the elements in Mexico, is best fitted to attack national problems with sympathetic understanding. He is best prepared to appreciate the need and the full significance of the cultural revolution inaugurated by the rural school.

The Mexican scene presents a complexity of culture contacts and conflicts. Indian and Spaniard, each representing not one cultural pattern but many, have joined the turbid waters of their respective cultural reservoirs to form the new stream that is Mexican life today. The *mestizo* symbolizes this new stream. There is much to support the assertion that Mexican culture is neither Indian nor Spanish but *mestizo*. This must be borne in mind in the study of Mexican institutions, for their fitness or adequacy cannot be judged properly without due regard for the fact that, whatever their origins, they now function in a society that is predominantly *mestizo*.

EUROPEAN INFLUENCES

Mention has already been made of the estimate which indicates that the number of Europeans in Mexico at any one time was less than two million. Molina Enríquez states that the Spaniards and *criollos* (American born whites) constituted less than 10 per cent of the population before 1821.[21] Gruening indicates that the white population of New Spain was only one-fifth of the total and that the number of Spaniards at the close of the colonial regime was but 15,000, "less than one-third of one per cent of the population of New Spain."[22]

All this leads to the conclusion that European influences in Mexico has been represented by an extremely small proportion of the population. Furthermore, it is apparent that, after the initial movement of Europeans to New Spain in the sixteenth century, contacts with the Western world were highly limited and that the basic pattern of European culture which formed the frame-work or background for Mexican developments was essentially that of sixteenth-century Spain. Because, since then, there has been no important movement of Europeans to this region, it follows that New Spain has been virtually isolated from and immune to the effects of the tremendous changes which were taking place in Europe. The importance of this consideration must not be underestimated for therein lies a factor of great significance to the interpretation of Mexican civilization.

Before looking into some of the elements which characterized the European contribution brought to New Spain by the conquerors and first settlers, it is well to emphasize the fact that by the end of the sixteenth century the foundations of all important social institutions had been laid. Permanent settlements had been founded as far north as San Juan de los Caballeros (north of Santa Fe) in New Mexico, and as far south and east as Yucatan and Central America. Monterrey, Guadalajara, and Villahermosa were thriving centers. Cities, towns, and villages, under Spanish control, dotted almost the entire central plateau. Vera Cruz and Acapulco were already important ports. The mining industry was well established

[21] Molina Enríquez, *op. cit.*, I, 72.
[22] Ernest Gruening, *Mexico and its Heritage* (New York, 1934), p. 23.

as was the basic pattern of colonial agriculture. Government had been given the structure that was to obtain for over two hundred years. The Church, likewise, had become well organized and firmly entrenched throughout New Spain. Thus, by 1600, New Spain had passed the exploratory period, had assumed its characteristic social and economic patterns, and offered little room for major innovations or changes in any of its fundamental structures or procedures. It was no longer a frontier, economically or socially. This being the case, the nature of the sixteenth-century European contribution takes on especial importance for the student of Mexican affairs.

Mexico was settled during the most flourishing era of Spanish culture. The period 1474–1659 saw Spain at the height of her glory. In letters and science, in government and economics, and in the very spirit which pervaded Spanish life at that time, Spain presented a picture of great achievements and progress. It was this Spain that came to America. As Don Fernando de los Ríos has stated: [23]

> Spain came to America integrally. She gave America as much as she had: political institutions, social and economic organization, cultural foundations, arts, religion. She came with her *Weltanschauung* and even with her internal drama, because as a people, as a nation, she did not show reserve in her actions, but exerted her full personality in each of her actions. . . .
>
> The will to power and the will to *imperium,* in the double dimension so loved by the Renaissance, material and spiritual, reached through Spain its apex.
>
> The conquistadores represent the most outstanding example of the will to power known at that tumultuous epoch of renascence. In that period of exaltation of individuals, of unlimited faith in the value of every human action, the appetite for power and glory is embodied in the conquistadores. Perhaps a comparable display of will has never been made in history. Thus we have the words of Nietzsche: "Spain, Spain is a people that has wanted too much," and he knew the essence of the will! The efficiency and elasticity of the individual will and the collective will of Spain then acquired proportions never before revealed; human limitations appeared to be overcome.

[23] Charles C. Griffin ed. *Concerning Latin American Culture.* Columbia University Press (For the National Committee of the United States of America on Intellectual Cooperation) (New York, 1940), pp. 52, 53.

Alongside this bright phase of the Spanish culture of that time, however, there were some less heartening features.[24] Absolutism, characteristic of most of Europe, was steadily growing in Spain and the royal power was supreme. The towns, the nobles, and even the *cortes* had been shorn of their powers and the dispensing of privilege was the prerogative of the Crown. Court favor was the acme of ambition, for therein rested the source of social and economic opportunity. Those who aspired to wealth and power sought royal goodwill, an office. The bureaucracy through which the Crown expressed its absolute powers was large and cumbersome. The King was the head of the Spanish Church, and the struggle with the Moors and the Jews, partly religious, partly political in character, had made that Church more repressive and reactionary than was the case elsewhere. Wealth and temporal power had made of the clergy a socially and economically privileged class in the prevailing class system. The secular clergy ranked with the aristocracy and was moved by the same worldly ambitions that motivated the lay nobility. The well-intentioned aims of benevolent monarchs and churchmen often went astray in the hands of a self-seeking officialdom or were so bound up in red tape that they never attained effective expression in practice, particularly in distant colonies. In New Spain, where even the little restraint offered by the *cortes* and the various councils in the homeland was non-existent, absolutism in government was even more pronounced than in the mother country. As Gruening says:[25]

> Conquest accomplished, the crown organized its new kingdom. Grandees alone were deemed worthy of administering it. The magnificence and power of absolute monarchy were delegated in New Spain to the viceroy. "He represents our royal person." As captain-general he was commander-in-chief of the kingdom's army and navy. As governor of the province he headed the civil administration. As president of the *Audiencia,* and in other capacities, he dispensed justice. He was superintendent of the royal treasury, responsible for augmenting, collecting, and transmitting the king's revenue. He published *bandos* or proclamations, enacting His Majesty's legislation sent through the Council of the Indies. He was vice-patron of the church. He exercised a great variety of lesser duties, filled many offices temporarily until the arrival of the

---

[24] *Ibid.,* pp. 34 ff.
[25] Gruening, *op. cit.,* pp. 15–16.

royal appointee, settled commercial disputes, concerned himself with public health and morals. His extra-official powers were enormous and his favor or displeasure could make or ruin all but the best-connected.

The above views are not offered to suggest that, for their time, conditions in Spain were unique in Europe nor to imply undue disparagement of Spanish achievements. Rather, these impressions are intended to serve merely as a reminder that the cultural scene from which the Conquest arose presented both liberal and reactionary tendencies—with the advantages and disadvantages which such a conflict of trends entailed. It is not undue criticism to point out that in some phases of life, sixteenth century Spain did not rise above the level of its European environment and did not transcend the standards of its age. As a matter of fact, an understanding of the handicaps of the milieu out of which Spain rose to greatness serves to bring out in bold relief those liberal, forward-looking views and achievements which formed a part of Spanish colonial endeavor. The social conditions in Spain, and the part which the law and clerical aristocracy played in a society in transition, were the background for numerous brilliant contributions by rulers, laymen, and clergymen. Further on, this study will describe some of these attainments in New Spain. However, it must be kept in mind constantly that the background was in a state of flux, that much of the social pattern for New Spain was designed under the limitations of medieval norms, and that it is in part by those norms that the foundations of social institutions in Mexico must be judged. This observation has particular importance in the light of these facts: (1) In the momentous sixteenth, seventeenth, and eighteenth centuries, instead of joining with northern Europe in the social and economic reforms arising out of the intellectual revolt against certain phases of medieval practices and ideology, Spain isolated herself and her colonies from contact with the streams of that revolt; and (2), as pointed out before, the contact of New Spain with the mother country, to say nothing of the prohibited contact with the rest of Europe, was virtually reduced to the exchange of church and governmental officials.

The intellectual environment of sixteenth-century Spain is worthy of note in a study of the backgrounds of Mexican institutions. It is unnecessary to review in detail here the characteristics of post-Renaissance southern Europe. It should be remembered, however, that the great impetus given to learning by the intellectual discoveries and interests of the four-

teenth and fifteenth centuries (and earlier still in Spain) was at its peak
in Italy and Spain at the time of the Conquest. The enlightened humanism
of Petrarch had not yet degenerated into structural formalism.

However, the centers of higher study, which in the fifteenth century
had reluctantly opened their doors to the new learning, were busy institu-
tionalizing humanism and were slowly converting it into a modified
scholasticism. At a time when the liberal energies of humanistic education
were being directed towards social ends and the advancement of morality
and religion elsewhere, the countries of southern Europe were reverting
to formal discipline and to narrow ecclesiastical doctrines and traditions.
It must be remembered, also, that humanism in the south was regarded
as leading towards personal development rather than towards social or
moral ends. This, together with the fact that the new subjects of study
formed the springboard for the Protestant Revolution, brought the new
learning into ill-favor with the Church. Thus we find that, in the Catholic
countries, France to some extent excepted, there developed in time a reaction against the old humanism to which they had given rise as well as
against the humanistic realism and the kind of realism which subsequently
evolved from it.

All these considerations add up to the general conclusion that, by the
end of the seventeenth century, Spain had withdrawn from the front ranks
of intellectual exploration and had cast its lot with a narrow and formal
humanism that was only a short step-removed from scholasticism. In this
way she not only insulated herself against the growing tide of religious
and political dissension sweeping northern Europe but she also isolated
her society from the benefits of the intellectual advances which were in
the making beyond her borders. By and large, both in Spain and in the
rest of Europe during the late seventeenth century, education remained
formal and aristocratic rather than liberal and popular, learning was
scholastic and *a priori* instead of humanistic and inductive. It is well to
remember at this point that the foundations of the scientific method as
represented by sense realism and the *Novum Organum,* and in the work
of such men as Newton, Descartes, Locke, and Comenius, were not laid
until after the sixteenth century. Post-sixteenth century learning in New
Spain, then, was not only established under the aegis of a culturally isola-
tionist nation and at a time when education everywhere was formal and
aristocratic, but it was sponsored during a period before the essential tools
that characterize the modern intellectual world were available. As will

become manifest later in this study, it is therefore all the more remarkable that, during the century following the Conquest, New Spain, in spite of its geographic and cultural isolation, was able to evolve progressive ideas and practices which, contemporaneously and subsequently, rivalled those of peoples under less restricted auspices.

This lengthy but far from complete exposition of the cultural scene sets forth some of the salient factors which have determined or conditioned the course of Mexican developments. While a more detailed presentation of the cultural elements involved would reveal many other significant features, this review makes palpable the complexity of the antecedents of Mexican social institutions. The unusual character of some of these antecedents and the peculiar nature of some of the basic elements out of which Mexican culture has arisen constitute the frame of reference for the development of education in Mexico. In judging that development it is indispensable that the student have an understanding of Mexican geography, of the peoples involved, and the historical period concerned. These are the factors which characterize a society. These factors are the bricks and mortar out of which educational goals and programs have arisen. The attainments of schools anywhere have little meaning except in terms of how well they have utilized the resources at hand and to what extent they have been able to overcome the handicaps which nature, man, and time have offered. The foregoing pages should make it clear that in Mexico, nature, man, and time have contributed an unusual combination of circumstances as that nation's background. It can confidently be expected that Mexican culture will reflect her unusual antecedents and that Mexican education follows patterns which can be evaluated only in terms of that heritage.

Chapter Two

EDUCATIONAL FOUNDATIONS

THE FOUNDING of educational institutions in New Spain was carried out at a time when Europe was undergoing a tremendous intellectual revolution. The history of Europe for the period 1450–1550, the period which constitutes the springboard for the Western influences affecting New Spain, is a history of momentous intellectual changes and of a portentous redirection of human interests. During this time the Western World was in the process of transition from its medieval age to the modern age, from the hoary norms of the longest and most intellectually conservative period in the history of Europe to the kaleidoscopic, swiftly moving world of today. This change of pace was accompanied by numerous epoch-making reforms in educational principles and practice, reforms which led away from the narrow intellectual horizons of the past to new frontiers of human values and conduct, of social endeavor and well-being.

These reforms were not born without conflict, however, nor were they achieved uniformly by European nations. The impetus of the Renaissance was variously felt and expressed, medievalism was not equally entrenched over the European scene, and social and economic circumstances varied from region to region. All this made the European intellectual milieu of this period highly complex. Even though the dominant trend was liberal and progressive, there were many cross-currents and eddies. These cross-currents and eddies gave the underlying flow of the stream of intellectual endeavor a turbid aspect and made its course uneven and erratic. The schools of New Spain stem from this uneven channeling of European culture-in-flux and many of their peculiarities are explained in the light of the fact that these schools had their origins in this highly unsettled period.

CULTURAL ANTECEDENTS AND THE SIXTEENTH CENTURY

Prior to 1519—that is, prior to the Conquest of Mexico—Spain and the Church were closely associated with every phase of the events and trends of this involved period. Not only that, but Spain held an eminent position in world affairs and could draw upon the best intellectual resources of Europe. Therefore we find Spanish leadership, in New Spain especially, expressing views and carrying on practices gleaned from the best thinking and experience of the entire contemporary Western World. After that time, it is noticeable that policy and leadership become much more restricted and sterile. The schools of New Spain reflect both these tendencies: the liberal one, carried out in the fervor of a widespread revival of learning that knew no national bounds and was not confined to sectarian norms, and the conservative which found its sanctions in the Spanish Church and State, confronted by revolt, political and religious.

During most of its first century, the destinies of the colony were in the hands of men whose source of inspiration had come from the world at large, unhampered by schismatic contentions in the religious sphere. Subsequently, the leadership in New Spain had to come from among conformists whose pattern of behavior and thought was prescribed by the changed outlook of the mother country and its Church and who looked with distrust upon educational innovations.

It is not within the province of this study to review the history of education of pre-sixteenth century Europe nor to analyze the effects of the subsequent parting of the ways between the Catholic and the Protestant worlds. It must not, therefore, be assumed that such study and analysis has little or only incidental bearing on the course of educational events in Mexico. Quite to the contrary, the student of Mexican education will find that a thorough knowledge of European affairs, educational and political, is a prerequisite to an understanding of the course of learning in Mexico. This is particularly true when the period during which the educational foundations were being laid in New Spain is under consideration.

The values of the medieval world form a significant part of those foundations. The Revival of Learning and Humanism comprised a wave which, at its crest in Spain at the time of the Conquest, poured on into the New World and cast some of its finest gems of intellectual fervor and acumen upon these shores. It needs to be kept in mind that the Revival of Learning in southern Europe was not simply a literary one. It was also artistic and emotional. While, as has been suggested before, it was not directed towards social ends but was highly individualistic, it was not necessarily selfish. It carried an underlying tone of appreciation for the "good, the true, and the beautiful," an appreciation which could easily be, and often has been, the motive for social reforms. The decline of Spain as a political and economic power, the shortening of her intellectual lines in defense of her faith and her lands against a growing tide of religious and political revolt, and her governmental absolutism played a leading role in shaping part of these foundations and in designing the structure that was to rest upon them for two hundred years. The study of European trends is, from this viewpoint, the point of departure for an evaluation of Mexican education.

The student of Mexican affairs is astonished at the striking change evidenced in education since the sixteenth century. The first eighty years of the colony constituted a truly golden age in its establishment of schools. Fervid initiative, a liberal social outlook, penetrating insight, and courageous endeavor characterize the educational scene of that period. Relatively speaking, and in sharp contrast, the next two centuries present a picture of educational stagnation and decay, of narrow institutionalism, of indifference to the goals of the school as a social institution. This remarkable change in the tone and tempo of education was a product of many factors. In the preceding chapter note has been made of some of the salient difficulties offered by the New World setting. In that chapter and in the preceding paragraphs of this one, it has been pointed out that the state of intellectual affairs in Spain, and in Europe as a whole, also had an important causal relationship to this radical change in Mexican educational trends.

The foundations of Mexican culture were established under the impetus of the favored position enjoyed by Spain in the early sixteenth century. It was at that time that the characteristics which have since distinguished Mexican peoples and the Mexican nation were first expressed. The culture contacts and conflicts of that period gave direction to the heterogeneous native peoples and to the newcomers from Europe. Without question, the influence exercised by European culture during the early years of the colony became the standard or base upon which future developments were to take place. As Paula Alegría says in her valuable study on education: [1]

> . . . The valuable educational work of the sixteenth century . . . may be considered as among the most brilliant in history, since it was in that century that the culture of New Spain blossomed. While it is true that at that time the seekers after gold, who stopped at nothing to obtain it, left their blot, it is necessary to have sufficient impartiality to know that,

[1] Paula Alegría, *La Educación En México Antes Y Después De La Conquista*. Mexico, Editorial "Cultura," 1936, pp. 85–86.

simultaneously, there came unselfish, generous, and noble men who understood the Indian and sought to educate him—true educators who, in the warlike lands of ancient Tenochtitlán as in other parts, were to carry on their constructive work, firm base for higher culture. . . . As the directing point for the light to come, they founded the first educational institutions through which Europe was to bequeath its culture to the newly discovered continent.

That beginning opened new paths to the native peoples and it gave a new meaning to European values. It was a demonstration of those courses of action which were to serve as the norms for future endeavor, give direction to cultural amalgamation and set social goals which, in the light of the times and the setting, cannot be regarded as other than inspired. The worth of the contributions made during the first century of the colony is to be judged not so much by material standards as by the ideas expressed and by the trends established. Wide-visioned laymen and churchmen, alike privately and under official auspices, valiantly struck out along new intellectual paths to bring enlightenment to the new lands, founding schools, writing and publishing books, patronizing the fine arts, organizing communities, and carrying on a multitude of other similar educational activities which rival the best that the learned world of Europe had to offer. These activities, carried out with full regard for the realities as well as the potentialities of the Mexican scene, embrace the cultural growth and development of Spaniards, Indians, and *mestizos*.

These efforts reveal a penetrating insight into and an appreciation of human values that either scarcely touched or were as yet outside the ken of contemporary Europe. More's *Utopia* (1516) was the expression of visionary hope—Quiroga's [2] *Hospitales* were real-life utopian communities less than twenty years later. Fray Alonso de la Veracruz rivals Erasmus as a scholar—to say nothing of Fray Alonso's activities in the founding and organization of schools. One would have to look to John Amos Comenius (1592-1670), the tragic Moravian bishop, to find an educator with whom to compare Fray Pedro de Gante, that saintly and tireless champion of Mexican education, the first educator of the New World. The fundamental principle that education is the only sound basis for the relief of the poor, exemplified in Europe in the laws of the Netherlands

[2] References and citations connected with Vasco de Quiroga, Alonso de la Veracruz, Pedro de Gante, and Zumárraga appear in later sections where their contributions are dealt with more specifically.

(1531) and in the writings of the great educational reformer, Juan Luís Vives (*De Subventione Pauperum*, 1526), was practiced in numerous instances before 1540 and also later under the sponsorship of Fray Juan de Zumárraga. The use of vernacular languages in education, ably pioneered in the Netherlands and Spain, and championed by Spanish scholars during the preceding century, was carried to new high levels when in Mexico, within a few years after the Conquest, Indian dialects were used as the medium of instruction in certain elementary schools, as the language for certain textbooks, and as subjects in the curricula of institutions of higher learning. Less than one hundred years after the invention of the printing press and less than fifty years after the discovery of America by Columbus, books were being published in Mexico as a result of the energy and foresight of Viceroy Mendoza and Archbishop Zumárraga (1468?–1548). No sooner had the Conquestion been complete than dramatic works and other forms of literature, rivalling even those of Spain during this, her literary golden age, appeared in New Spain. Thus, reading between the lines of history, we may judge of the true worth of the sixteenth century and appreciate the full significance of the men of that century in the development of Mexican culture.

LIBERAL LAY LEADERSHIP

These events represent achievements that redound not only to the credit of the Church and its clergy but also to the glory of the ruling laymen. The close relationship between State and Church, and the governmental absolutism already referred to, might well have frustrated these progressive trends and attainments had there not been a few elements in the lay nobility of both Spain and New Spain that deserve to rank in the vanguard of liberal leadership. In judging their contributions it should be kept in mind that they acted within a social structure that was most unfavorable to freedom of action and thought. That structure, military and theocratic in character by its absolutism, circumscribed all behavior and with its narrow regulations, reached out to control every act of life. Furthermore, in New Spain, that absolutism was complicated by the anarchic scramble for power, privilege, and wealth by those adventurers who felt that their personal part in the Conquest had vested them with rights over the human and material resources of the new lands. It is, therefore, all the more remarkable that there were men who rose above the dictates of personal gain and narrow imperialism to play the part of Christian gentlemen and enlightened statesmen.

The dauntless and much maligned Cortés himself deserves a tribute for what he did to open the doors to learning and progress. Priestley acknowledges this when he says: [3]

The conquest thus partook of two characters, temporal and spiritual. It would be difficult to decide which aspect of the problem was entered into, at first, with the greater zest and enthusiasm. Throughout the sixteenth century at least the Spaniards were as zealous in proselytizing as they were avid for conquest and riches. The church was no whit behind the lusty conquistadores in improving its opportunities. And though religion and morals, religion and humanitarianism, were sharply divorced in the minds of the military campaigners, they were strongly united in the minds and purposes of the sovereigns; and their spiritual agents the churchmen were imbued with the same principles. The idealism of the church was eminently practical for its age; it strove for wide and prompt conversions; the fathers even coveted the oft-received crown of martyrdom at the hands of the savages in their all too scantily appreciated apostolates.

The conquestion of Mexico fell into the hands of a man of peculiarly intense piety. . . . The great conqueror felt that he was ordained of heaven to accomplish the spread of holy religion; he even cherished the belief that his military successes were achieved because of the sacred motto, "The Holy Cross is our banner, and under it we shall conquer," under which he essayed his great enterprise. He even proclaimed the spiritual conquest to be the primary motive of his campaigns, and declared that without it his temporal conquests would be unjust.[4]

Hence it is not strange that he took prompt means to further the cause of Christianity. No sooner had Tenochtitlán fallen than he began to seek from Spain the spiritual assistants needed to carry on the labor of conversions for which his army chaplains had been inadequate.

It is known that Cortés was not in sympathy with the practices of the secular clergy in Spain, yet he was anxious that clergyman be sent to New Spain to assist in the incorporation of the Indians. One of his first

[3] Herbert Priestley, *The Mexican Nation* (New York, 1930), pp. 96–97.
[4] Cf. William H. Prescott, *Conquest of Mexico*.

acts after the conquestion of Mexico City was to petition the King of Spain to send clergymen who would devote themselves to the instruction and conversion of the natives. In his request, Cortés expressed preference for the regular clergy since he doubted the wisdom of utilizing the secular clergy for these purposes. In this connection, Gruening says: [5]

> With remarkable foresight Cortés less than three years after the Conquest had urged the sending to New Spain of clergy of "exemplary and virtuous life," saying that the propagation of the faith would be injured and little serviceable to the natives if
>
>> the bishops and other prelates do not abandon the custom that on account of our sinfulness they pursue today of disposing of the goods of the church, spending them in pomp and other vices and leaving inheritances to their *sons* and relatives; and this would be the worse because the natives' own priests versed in their rites and ceremonies were chosen both for their honesty and chastity, deviation from which was punished by death; and if the natives saw church matters and the service of God in the hands of canons and other dignitaries, and knew these to be engaged in the vices and profanities which have been their wont in our times and kingdom, it would not only mock our faith and greatly damage it, but cause scant attention to be paid to its preachments. (From a letter written from Mexico by Hernán Cortés to Emperor Charles V, October 15, 1524—the so-called 4th letter. Biblioteca de Autores Españoles, vol. XXII, p. 115.)

Thus it was that, at the insistence of Cortés, the early friars came to New Spain to perform their memorable service to Mexican culture. It should be recognized, also, that it was Cortés who sponsored the education of Indian leaders to qualify them for posts in the civil government of the colony. Paula Alegría has this to say of it: [6]

> In the school of San José de Belen de los Naturales there was another type of student, made up of the sons of the great lords, who were trained in civic affairs so that they would discharge efficiently the governmental positions which had been reserved to them from the very beginning by the Spaniards. As Fray Pedro himself indicates, judges, mayors, and town trustees were educated there. Thus he (Fray Pedro) seconded Cortés' purpose which, as was expressly made clear to Charles V, had

---

[5] Gruening, *op. cit.*, pp. 173–174. [6] Alegría, *op. cit.*, p. 102.

this as its aim: to bring about the material and spiritual reconstruction of Tenochtitlán by utilizing the native peoples. Cortés with his characteristic perspicacity appreciated the necessity not only of confiding to them the rough material labor but also of sharing the government with them in order to obtain more effective results. The teachings of Fray Pedro contributed notably in the establishment of this form of shared government which was organized in all towns, giving impetus to the assimilation of Hispanic culture by the conquered peoples.

Cortés, that crusty and resourceful warrior, is thereby shown to have tempered his sternness and ambition with a measure of liberal vision and a feeling for social values. That he, the symbol of conquest and a ruthless age, should respond to the dictates of humanitarianism to that extent betokens the bringing to New Spain of some of the finest features of Spanish enlightenment, an enlightenment which was already growing fainter in the mother country. Nor was Cortés' interest in social reforms out of character. It was in close accord with the spirit that permeated the best of that leadership with which Spanish culture, at its height and on the verge of its decline, endowed its chosen offspring in America.

An illustration of how this spirit could influence the early years of New Spain is given us by Castañeda in his description of "the first charitable institution." [7]

On March 16, 1538, a group of socially minded Spaniards gathered in the monastery of San Francisco to discuss conditions of poverty and need in Mexico. As a result of that meeting the Brotherhood of the Blessed Sacrament came into existence, dedicated to the service of mankind. The 23 charter members drew up a constitution and defined their purposes. . . .

Prominent among the names of the members of the Brotherhood is that of Francisco Vásquez de Coronado. . . . Among the members, too, were men who had served under Cortez, Pedrarias, Ayllon, and Narvaez.

A list of the purposes of the Brotherhood reads like those of a modern organization. [They were]: to give assistance to the needy, to visit and care for the sick, to visit and provide food for prisoners, to assist needy widows, and to educate orphan girls . . .

[7] C. E. Castañeda, "These Things Began in Mexico," *Today and Tomorrow* (discontinued), March 1, 1941, pp. 28–29.

Today, several American welfare societies share the problems of caring for impoverished immigrants. Four hundred years ago the Brotherhood of the Blessed Sacrament also was stirred with pity for the need of the new arrivals from Europe. In the financial records of the Brotherhood may be found numerous references to the activities of representatives sent to meet flotillas of ships arriving at Vera Cruz—one representative to each flotilla. This representative had the authority to buy food and necessities for any sick or needy travelers.

The influence that both the golden age of Spanish letters and missionary zeal had upon New Spain is brought out by Castañeda when writing of his translation of "the first American play." [8] He says:

Thus almost two hundred years before the first play was given in Williamsburg, Virginia, dramatic representations were common in Mexico City. It was only natural that the Spaniards should have introduced, from the earliest days of the Conquest, the observance of practices connected with their religious festivals in Spain, given their fervent faith and the fact that, in spite of the general belief that their prime motive throughout the heroic age of exploration was sordid gain, they were swayed as strongly by a crusading spirit fostered by more than seven hundred years of constant warfare against the infidels in their own country.

One needs to keep in mind that the sixteenth century was the golden age of Spanish literature; that it was at this time that Spain was not only the most powerful nation in Europe but also the champion of the Church under the leadership of Charles V; that the theater in Spain reached its highest development during this period and produced such dramatists as Lope de Vega, Tirso de Molina and Calderón de la Barca; that the new colony in North America gave evidence from the very first years of a hardy literary development, and by the close of the century contributed to Spanish letters one of its leading lights, Juan Ruíz de Alarcón; and lastly, that it was during this century that the *auto,* a form of the religious or theological play was fully developed in Spain. With such antecedents the development of religous and pseudo-religous plays in New Spain from the earliest years of the Conquest is but a logical sequence.

[8] C. E. Castañeda, "The First American Play," *Preliminary Studies of the Texas Catholic Historical Society,* Volume III, Number 1, January 1, 1936, pp. 5-6.

The liberal social outlook of the lay leadership of this period is reflected in the achievements of the First Viceroy (1535-1550), Antonio de Mendoza, who "belonged to the military order of Santiago, had been a successful ambassador to Rome, was a cousin of the archbishop of Seville and cardinal of Spain, and was, by blood, connected with Spanish royalty." [9] Commenting on a scathing indictment of the viceroys and archbishops, Teja Zabre, who normally finds little to commend in the Spaniards, has this to say of Mendoza and of "the Emancipator," Luís de Velasco, the Second Viceroy: [10]

This (wholesale indictment) is an exaggeration, but only as regards such men as Antonio de Mendoza and Luís de Velasco, who were famous for their administrative ability, their lofty regard for humanity and their innate honesty and dignity. They stood for the desire of the Spanish Crown to save Indian races from absolute extinction or unmitigated slavery, and the formation of a state which would establish a balance between the privileged classes and the impoverished masses.

Mendoza was a real patron of learning and social welfare. He gave energetic support to the educational and charitable work being done by the clergy, and exerted unfailing pressure to bring about the creation of new institutions of learning. It was he who, largely at his own expense, founded the first real institution of higher learning in the New World— the Colegio de Santa Cruz de Tlatelolco, the Indian school which will be referred to later. His unchanging pressure brought about the founding of the Real y Pontificia Universidad de México. He and his successor Velasco, who like him was both a Knight of Santiago and also connected with royalty, were tireless in spreading the best of Spanish civilization throughout New Spain. Their devotion to a true spirit of liberal culture left its indelible imprint in the form of schools for all sectors of the population, hospitals and other charitable institutions, the impetus it gave to printing, to crafts and commerce, and to good government. Scholarship and social service flourished under their patronage and collaboration. Credit for the attainment of this golden age of Mexican culture should be ascribed to them as well as to the great clerical figures of the period. For comparable achievements by rulers one must look to a much later day in European history. These men exemplify Spanish leadership at its best, cast upon these shores as the flower of Spanish humanism was beginning to fade and wither.

[9] Priestley, *op. cit.*, p. 54.
[10] Alfonso Teja Zabre, *Guide to the History of Mexico* (Mexico, Press of the Ministry of Foreign Affairs, 1935), p. 162.

THE PRESS AND BOOKS

Probably no single event is so symbolic of the favor with which learning was viewed in New Spain as the introduction of the printing press. This contribution to education has been ably reviewed by Castañeda.[11] There was a press in Mexico as early as 1534, and large-scale printing began in 1539 when a branch of a Seville printing firm was established in Mexico as a result of the efforts of Archbishop Zumárraga and the active interest of Viceroy Mendoza. It was not long before another press appeared and, by 1600, 234 items had been printed. "The bulk of the production," says Castañeda in the articles cited above, "particularly in the early years, was made up of works on Christian doctrine, catechisms, and books of religious instruction. Equally notable are the Indian grammars, vocabularies, and dictionaries of the languages spoken by the various tribes of Mexico, which today form such a rich repository for the study of native linguistics. In this type should also be included the numerous *confesionarios, doctrinas,* and other books of instruction written in the native languages to aid the missionaries and natives alike. In addition to the books that fall into these two groups, we find others on theology, philosophy, hagiography, medicine, history, psalters, rituals, sermons, songbooks, psalmody, missals, law, military science, nautical instruction, and arithmetic." Among the publications listed by Castañeda are to be found the following which are of special interest to the student of education. Copies of those marked * are in the Library of the University of Texas:

> 1544—The oldest book in the New World, Bishop Zumárraga's *Doctrina Breve*. While it is known that other items had issued from the press in Mexico before that date, either there are no copies of them extant or only fragments have come down to this day, the *Doctrina Breve* being the oldest complete book extant.
>
> 1554—*Commentaria in Ludovici Vives* (Juan Luís Vives) *Exercitationes Linguae Latinae,* literary essays by Francisco Cervantes de Salazar, professor of rhetoric at the University of Mexico.
>
> 1554—In this year Fray Alonso de la Veracruz, the brilliant humanist whose outstanding scholarship was matched by his ability as a founder

[11] C. E. Castañeda, "Beginnings of Printing in America," *Preliminary Studies Of The Texas Catholic Historical Society,* Volume III, Number 7, November, 1940 (reprint from *The American Historical Review,* Volume XX, Number 4, November, 1940).
———— "The First Printing Press in Mexico," *The Publishers' Weekly,* January 6, 1940, pp. 50–53.

of colleges, published two textbooks, the *Recognitio Summularum* and the *Dialectica resolutio cum textu Aristotelis*. Three years later, in 1557, he published his *Phisica speculatio*. Thus, to this distinguished professor of the University of Mexico goes the credit for the first book of science and for the first books on philosophy and logic in the New World. These books were reprinted and widely used in Spain.

1555—The first dictionary, *Vocabulario en la lengua castellana y mexicana*, written by the Augustinian, Alonso de Molina, who, in 1546, had published a *Doctrina Christiana breve en lengua Mexicana*. His *Vocabulario* and *Doctrina*, in the Mexican language (Nahuatl—the language of the Aztecs), show the importance given to the vernacular in New Spain as is further evidenced by the existence of several other dictionaries and *doctrinas* in other native languages as well as in Nahuatl. While Castañeda credits Molina with the first *doctrina* in a native language, Paula Alegría [12] states (1) that Fray Pedro de Gante's *Doctrina Christiana en Lengua Mexicana* had been published in Flanders in 1528 and later reprinted in Mexico and that the Augustinians had adopted it as a text; and (2) that Zumárraga, in 1539, had published in Mexico (as his own, or as written under his auspices) a "Breve y más compendiosa doctrina cristiana en lengua mexicana, que contiene las más necesarias de nuestra fe católica, para aprovechamiento de estos indios naturales y salvación de sus ánimas." The Dominicans had a *Doctrina Christiana en lengua Española y Mexicana* in 1550.

1570—The first book on medicine in America, that of Doctor Francisco Bravo, *Opera Medicinalia in qbus qz plurina extantcitu medico necessaria . . ."* In 1578 Dr. Alonso López de Hinojoso published his *Summa y Recopilación de Chirugía*, the first book on surgery.

1579—*De constructione octo partium Orationis,* the first Latin grammar, published by a Jesuit priest, Manuel Alvarez.

The above list is, in effect, a flattering commentary on the level of learning and the scholarly interests of the colony. It is to be noted, also, that these books were not only learned treatises but they were works of art of a higher order. The beauty and artistry inherent in them, indeed, the fine craftsmanship which they display, and the effort and perseverance which they evince reveal the unusual quality of the culture which was in the

[12] Alegría, *op. cit.,* pp. 113–114, 194–195.

making—wherein aesthetics was a vital element of erudition. These works also symbolize the zeal with which intellectuals of the day seized upon the printing press, not as an instrument for the easy reproduction of Old World texts, but as a means for the expression of colonial research and scholarship. One cannot but view with admiration the original contributions made in the field of Indian languages, the intellectual freedom manifest in the works on science and philosophy, and the new, American, outlook which all of this implies. It is not to be supposed that European works were unavailable. In 1528 Fray Juan de Zumárraga had brought to Mexico a library of almost two hundred volumes to which he continued adding through the years. These books became the library of the Franciscans upon his death in 1548. Fray Alonso de la Veracruz imported an extensive collection of books, maps, and globes in 1574. With these he founded the library of the Colegio de San Pablo. Undoubtedly, other learned men of the times had their collections of European works.

THE CREATIVE SPIRIT

All of this emphasizes the fact that the Conquest of Mexico had a spiritual as well as a temporal aspect. That has often been stated. What has been overlooked is that, permeating both the temporal and the spiritual aspects and imbuing them with a unity which characterized the best elements in the foundations of Mexican culture, there was a *third aspect*—one that is reflected in a devotion to learning, in a zest for intellectual discovery, in the exploration of the unknown, and in the solution of difficult problems. This creative spirit, this fervid drive of the frontiersman, this zest for accomplishment transcended the dictates of religious doctrine and material gain. This was, indeed, the heroic age of Spanish history, an age in which the spirit of adventure was clothed in the finest robes of the southern Renaissance. True, this spirit did not motivate all lay and religious leaders in New Spain nor did it survive the century. Yet all evidence points to its widespread influence in the early years, the foundation years. Only thus can we explain events and achievements which transpired or were attained beyond, or without reference to, the normal obligations that might have been felt towards self, Church, or State.

The history of Mexican education before the nineteenth century is, largely, the story of the educational efforts of the clergy. During the entire colonial period, every process of life was closely associated with the activity of the Church. Education, morals, art, and, in short, all intellectual expression was within its sphere of interest, and the Church exercised control over the whole range of the realm of learning. In addition, the clergy was part and parcel of government and of economic endeavor. This means that, to a high degree, cultural trends in Mexico prior to the nineteenth century simply reflect the scope and temper of church interests and endeavor. It also means that, in subsequent periods, social and economic reforms have been conditioned by the traditions established under the auspices of the Church. Unfortunately, but quite understandably, the nineteenth and twentieth centuries have had to struggle against patterns of thought established during the seventeenth and eighteenth centuries, a period when the Church was most conservative and intolerant and during which it was least active in the field of social welfare and enlightenment. However, it must be remembered that the sixteenth century is also a part of the Mexican tradition and that the achievements of that period are no less a part of church history because they were characterized by a liberal spirit than those of later years which were deformed by less attractive characteristics.

A brief review of sixteenth-century religion is offered by Priestley.[13] The extent of church effort during this period is little short of amazing. By the end of the century there were in Mexico about 1,000 Franciscans, 600 Dominicans, 800 Augustinians, 400 Jesuits, and 450 friars representing other regular orders of the clergy.[14] Seventy-five years after the Conquest they had established some 400 convents (Franciscans 166, Dominicans 90, Augustinians 76, other regular orders about 68).[15] In addition there were about 400 parishes under the care of the secular clergy. The achievements of these men, particularly in the field of education, testify to a liberal viewpoint and to a dynamic spirit that is in sharp contrast to the patterns of thought and action to be observed in later periods. With proper regard for the time and place of these activities and with due appreciation of existing cultural limitations, this century is one of the brightest eras in church history and a monument to her energy and intelligence.

SIXTEENTH CENTURY COLLEGES

One cannot approach the history of higher education in Mexico without speaking at length of Fray Pedro de Gante (1480–1572), the father of education in the New World.[16] While his activities belong properly in the

[13] Priestley, *op. cit.*, pp. 96–114.   [14] Alegría, *op. cit.*, p. 83.   [15] Gruening, *op. cit.*, p. 174.
[16] For a summary of his work see:
Irma Wilson, *Mexico, a Century of Educational Thought.* New York, Hispanic Institute in the United States, 1941. pp. 16–17.

field of elementary education, he is the precursor of realism in Mexican learning and it was he who inaugurated secondary education.

The first school in the Americas was that founded for Indian children by Fray Pedro at Texcoco in 1523. It was there that he began to study the language of the natives and initiated his progressive methods of instruction. Fray Pedro, like most of the Franciscans who came later, immediately recognized that education should not be limited to children or to religious doctrine. Faced with the task of transforming the native culture and of building a new social order, they were impressed by the need for a broader and more realistic program of education, one that would reach the entire population and that would serve as a guide to civil as well as religious behavior. Thus, responding to the demands of the new environment, they undertook a program of education which was remarkable for its realism and foresightedness. This program, inaugurated on a small scale at Texcoco by Fray Pedro, spread everywhere that the Franciscans went. Almost invariably, their churches were planned to provide an annex and grounds for school purposes. The schools were usually residence schools. In addition to the instruction carried on in these schools, classes were offered to non-resident students—adults as well as children—in open-air meetings held on the church grounds. In the light of the broad purposes of education which they recognized, the Franciscans did not ignore the education of girls and, in these open-air classes, gave instruction to girls as well as boys. In addition, they were active in encouraging the establishment of schools and orphanages for girls.

Fray Pedro left Texcoco and settled in the City of Mexico early in 1527. By 1529 we find him conducting his great Indian school, San José de Belen de Los Naturales, in that city, and there he remained until his death in 1572, after almost half a century of outstanding educational services to New Spain.

The Colegio de San José de Belen was a remarkable institution. Not only did Fray Pedro resort to the vernacular (Nahuatl) as the medium of instruction but his program soon made the teaching of both Spanish and Latin necessary! Recognizing the important part that music and the dance had played in native culture, he seized upon them as a means of inculcating Christian doctrines. The use of this method of motivation as well as the need of expanding religious teaching led to the study of Spanish.

Sánchez, op. cit. (Mexico—A Revolution. . . .), pp. 37–39.
A more detailed study is offered by Ezequiel A. Chávez, El Primero de los Grandes Educadores de la América, Fray Pedro de Gante. Mexico, Imprenta Mundial, 1934.

Phonetic values were sometimes illustrated with hieroglyphics. The teaching of Spanish meant instruction in European matters. Interest in music led to the singing of religious songs in Latin and the study of that language. Thus we find that one of Fray Pedro's colleagues, Arnaldo de Basaccio, was the first to teach the Indians Latin grammar. And so the curriculum grew. Friars and students learned to make and play both European and autochthonous musical instruments. It has already been noted that some of the students were given an education that prepared them for posts in civil government. The making of church images and ornaments brought about the opening of a department of fine arts where embroidery, sculpture, and painting were taught. In addition, instruction in various trades—shoemaking, carpentry, tailoring, etc.—was a part of the program. The monitorial system of mutual instruction was developed to expand the scope of the influence of the friars, and some of the students were prepared to serve as teachers at San José, in neighboring parishes, and in nearby towns.

From the above sketch it will be apparent that this school was more than an elementary school. San José de Belen de los Naturales reached out to children, adolescents, and adults in fields of instruction ranging from reading, writing, and handicrafts to the fine arts, Latin grammar, and pedagogy. The most striking feature of the program was that Fray Pedro and his assistants not only had an eminently sound conception of the psychology of teaching and learning but they also had a phenomenal insight into the process of acculturation. Because of this, their work presaged the birth of a new, a Mexican culture. European patterns were interpreted in native ways and adjusted to native means, giving a Mexican character to European art and music, and to European techniques and structures. Fray Pedro, the tireless founder of a new school, appears then as more than merely a brilliant and humanitarian teacher. He envisioned a new culture as well and set about directing its first expressions. In doing that, he pointed the way for those who were to follow and create institutions of higher learning for his beloved Indians and *mestizos* as well as for the children of his fellow Europeans. For sheer educational daring, there is little in the history of education that is so thrilling as the educational adventures of this humble man, a lay friar who was of royal blood and who once refused the Archbishopric of Mexico,[17] who, with penetrating in-

[17] Alegría, *op. cit.*, pp. 87–89.
Chávez, *op. cit.*, pp. 79, 101.

sight and unswerving endeavor, gave a new direction to education and laid the cornerstone of Mexican culture.

The success of Fray Pedro's school is reflected in the founding in Mexico City in 1536 of the Colegio de Santa Cruz de Tlatelolco, an institution of higher learning for Indians less than two decades after the taking of the city by Cortés.[18] A royal order of December 8, 1535 had instructed the Viceroy, Don Antonio de Mendoza, that special attention be given to the education of Indians. In response to that order, and with the active co-operation of Archbishop Zumárraga, Mendoza founded the college, an institution that he endowed with some of his private holdings. As early as 1526, Charles V had given orders that a number of the sons of Indian nobles should be sent to Spain for higher education. Though this was not done, the interest in the higher training of Indians persisted and the opening of the new college on January 6, 1536, was an occasion of much gratification to those who had been so active in the promotion of education for the Indians.

The school opened with about sixty students, of from ten to twelve years of age, who had already been trained in elementary subjects. As has been indicated above, the school of San José had offered Indian students a broad education which included Latin grammar. The Colegio de Santa Cruz had a curriculum comprising religion, reading, writing, Latin, rhetoric, Indian medicine, music, and philosophy. The program of the school was divided into two cycles: an elementary program, similar to the one offered at San José, based on Christian doctrine and reading and writing in Spanish; a secondary program, embracing Latin grammar and literature, logic, philosophy, and science. The course in Indian medicine was based on the empirical hygienic practices of the Indians, their use of herbs and the like. In addition, those studying for religious orders received instruction in Indian languages.

The first rector of the college was the noted historian, Fray Bernardino de Sahagún (1499?-1590). It is of interest to note that, among his writings, Fray Bernardino included a tri-lingual dictionary—in Spanish, Latin, and Nahuatl. His *Historia de las Cosas de la Nueva Espana* is a monumental work on the life and events of that period. Fray Bernardino was an enthusiastic supporter of Indian education and he gave his support to

[18] C. E. Castañeda, *Nuevos Documentos Inéditos O Muy Raros Para La Historia De México.* Mexico, Talleres Gráficos de la Nación, 1929, pp. 1–8.

Tomás Zepeda Rincón, *La Instrucción Pública En La Nueva España En El Siglo XVI.* Mexico, Universidad Nacional de México, 1933, pp. 69–79.

the education of Indians for positions of trust and responsibility. It is known that in 1572 the rector of the college was an Indian, Martín Jacobita. This illustrates the success of the institution in the education of Indian leaders. A number of distinguished teachers of Indian languages and of other subjects graduated from this institution and several of them became teachers in the college. One was Antonio Valeriano who was an outstanding scholar in Latin, logic, and philosophy. Later he served as Governor of Mexico for forty years. It was this same Valeriano who translated Cato and who helped Fray Alonso de Molina in the preparation of his dictionary of the Mexican language. As Irma Wilson says: [19]

> Eminent men did the teaching: Arnaldo de Basaccio, who had taught Latin previously to the Indians in the Convent of Saint Francis in Mexico; García de Cisneros, one of the twelve Franciscans who came in 1524 and first provincial of his order in Mexico; Andrés de Olmos, the polyglot missionary; Juan de Gaona and Juan de Focher, former students of the University of Paris, the latter having a doctorate in laws from that institutions; Francisco de Bustamante, the first preacher of his time; and Bernardino de Sahagún, a philologist and historian, author of the *Historia general de las cosas de Nueva España*. Out of this college came the native *alcaldes*, governors, and teachers for the Indians and youthful Spaniards and *criollos*, who perhaps received from them the first direction that led them later to important posts in the church.

In spite of its evident success, the Colegio de Santa Cruz soon encountered serious opposition from both lay and official quarters. There were those who felt that Indian education was the cause of unrest and rebellion and that, therefore, the school should be abandoned. Not only that, but there is evidence that suggests that the Spaniards were envious of the distinction being attained by Indian scholars who, in some cases, became their teachers and knew Latin and higher studies better than they did. Though the institution was courageously defended by Sahagún and others, it can be said that it had disappeared by the end of the sixteenth century. This school has the undisputed distinction of having been not only the first institution of higher learning for Indians but the first institution of higher learning in the New World.

The work of don Vasco de Quiroga in the sixteenth century constitutes one of the most fascinating pages in Mexican history. Don Vasco was born

[19] Wilson, *op. cit.*, p. 20.

in Spain twenty-two years before the discovery of America.[20] As a member of a distinguished family he received a good higher education and became a highly successful jurist. His accomplishments in law brought him to the attention of the rulers of Spain and, at the age of sixty, he was designated one of the five members of the royal Audiencia in New Spain, where he arrived in 1531. Thus, after a normal lifetime of distinguished work in Spain, don Vasco undertook an imposing task in the New World where he served for thirty-five years. He died in 1565 when on one of his journeys of service and devotion among his beloved Tarascans, at the age of ninety-five.

Don Vasco de Quiroga was an important factor in the laying of the cultural foundations of Mexico.[21] At the very outset, as a member of the Audiencia, he became interested in the condition of the native peoples and, in 1532, founded his Hospital de Santa Fe, two leagues from Mexico City, where he established a community of some twelve thousand people. Around this hospital, which cared for the needy and sick as well as for foundlings, he organized a community-action program which embraced all popular activities. He opened a school, known as El Colegio de San Nicolás (not to be confused with San Nicolás Obispo, the college he founded later at Pátzcuaro), for the instruction of Indian children in reading, writing, singing, and instrumental music. In addition, he operated what may be regarded as the first nursery school in the New World. The land was worked in common, crops were stored in a common granary, everybody worked according to his ability, and, in effect, village life was communistic. Everything from the nursery school to the selection of the governing authorities was carried out cooperatively. Don Vasco's concept of Christianity was highly pragmatic, for his criteria for the good life were not limited to those of doctrine or dogma but were based on social action and useful living. Quiroga can be regarded as the father of Mexican rural education. He and Fray Pedro de Gante are the two great precursors of the educational reform movement of the twentieth century.

In 1533 he was sent to Michoacán where the Tarascan Indians were in need of assistance. Soon after his arrival there he founded another Hospital de Santa Fe at Pátzcuaro. It was there also that, in 1540, he established

[20] Consult: Rafael Aguayo Spencer, ed., *Don Vasco De Quiroga* (Mexico, Editorial Polis, 1940), pp. 19–20.

Pablo G. Macías, *Aula Nobilis*. Morelia, Michoacán, Mexico, Monografía del Colegio Primitivo y Nacional de San Nicolás de Hidalgo. 1940, pp. 60–64.

[21] Zepeda Rincón, *op. cit.*, pp. 59–68.

the Colegio de San Nicolás Obispo, an institution which will be discussed in detail in the following chapter. In 1537, at the age of 67, he was made Bishop of Michoacán, having been advanced rapidly upward through his religious orders since, prior to this time, he had taken only the minor ones. Bishop Vasco de Quiroga looms as the outstanding teacher and benefactor of the Tarascan peoples. It was he who introduced many of the crafts and lesser industries that have since characterized the life of the natives of that region. He gave each village its special trade, complementing the work done in one village with that of some nearby town. Through his efforts European music and art were absorbed by the Indians to the point that, today, Tarascan airs still retain qualities traceable to the European music of the time. The stimulation that Don Vasco gave to the development of Indian leadership has made the Tarascan people a highly important factor in the development of the Mexican nation. Many notable leaders have arisen from among them. Irma Wilson summarizes Quiroga's contribution and views as follows: [22]

Vasco de Quiroga (1470–1567), who was named *oidor* [judge] of New Spain in 1530 and was a member of the second audiencia, performed some social experiments in behalf of the native people which still exert an influence in the industrial life of some sections of the country. He founded his first *hospital-pueblo,* a community center, which he called Santa Fe, at a distance of some two leagues from Mexico. Shortly afterwards, in 1533, while *visitador* to Michoacán, he established another center with the same name, in Atamataho. In 1537 he became bishop of Michoacán, where he continued his work of incorporating the Indians in a social organization along communistic lines. None of the later foundations, however, attained the importance of the first two. Quiroga, who was well versed in the law, theology, and traditional culture of his time, was influenced in his projects for the Indians by Plato's *Republic,* which he received through Saint Cyril, by the *Saturniales* of Lucian, and by the *Utopia* of Thomas More, according to Silvio A. Zavala, in his recent study entitled *La "Utopia" de Tomás Moro en la Nueva España.* The first work supported the theory of community life, the second gave him the picture of the Golden Age with which he insistently compared the life of the Indian, and the third furnished the model of the organization of the communities compatible with the innocence that he found in the aborigines. The native peoples were ideally conditioned for developing a perfect state, untarnished as they were by the vices of greed and ambition. The responsibility of the Spanish government consisted in cherishing the virtues of the Indian and teaching him what he was lacking for his temporal and spiritual life.

Quiroga developed his foundations on two fundamental principles, obedience to laws and the dignity of labor. Once the people had selected their leaders, they were obliged to follow their orders. Every inhabitant of the center learned a trade in addition to the occupation of agriculture, which he began to acquire in his childhood.

Like Zumárraga, Quiroga believed in the education of both boys and girls, for whom he planned a practical instruction set in a background of Christian doctrine.

Vasco de Quiroga is best known for the work that he did in founding and organizing his Hospitales de Santa Fe, near Mexico City and Pátzcuaro, and for the broad social program and the far-reaching economic reforms which, in connection with those and other similar foundations, he instituted among the Indians. These activities are described in detail in the compilation made by Rafael Aguayo Spencer, previously cited. That compilation also reproduces the ordinances drawn up by Vasco de Quiroga for the operation of the *Hospitales*. Had Don Vasco limited his work in Mexico simply to his functions in the *Audiencia,* he would still hold an important place in the history of Mexico. The work that he did in rehabilitating and orienting indigenous populations, particularly those of what is now the state of Michoacán, is of transcendent significance in the entire picture of cultural development in Mexico. In this work he laid the foundations of rural education in Mexico and established the basis for the acculturation of the native peoples. Culture in the state of Michoacán today rests firmly, and consciously, upon the groundwork laid by the venerable bishop four hundred years ago. Modern-day intellectuals of that region recognize him as the outstanding figure of the colonial period. To the Tarascan Indian, he is still "Tata" Vasco, that great benefactor who still lives on in the memory of the common people and who is still their guiding spirit.

The first Augustinians arrived in Mexico in 1533 and they were soon engaged in the founding of convents and centers of secondary and higher education, largely in and near Mexico City and in what are now the states of Michoacán and Morelos. The National Library of Mexico is now housed in what was their principal convent in Mexico City. Their most famous schools were the Colegio de Tiripitío, in Michoacán, and the Colegio de San Pablo in Mexico City.[23] As was the case with both the Franciscans and the Dominicans, however, certain higher studies, primarily the liberal arts and theology, were made available in several of their convents which, before the close of the century, numbered seventy-six.

The Colegio de Tiripitío was founded in 1540 at their convent in the town of that name in Michoacán. Fray Alonso de la Veracruz (1504–1584) was sent to organize the program of studies which embraced the conventional disciplines of the higher education of the times. The school was meant to be a center of higher studies for the theological students of the Augustinians. Fray Alonso, who was a graduate of the University of Salamanca, taught the liberal arts and theology. To this school came a number of students who were to distinguish themselves later as church officials, as professors in the Royal and Pontifical University of Mexico, and as scholarly writers. Fray Alonso himself became the first professor of theology and dean of that faculty in the latter institution. One of his students at Tiripitío, who was also one of the first students at the University of Mexico, replaced him as the professor of theology at the Royal and Pontifical University. This same student, Pedro Agurto, was named Rector of the Colegio de San Pablo, an institution of higher learning which Fray Alonso, then Provincial of his Order, founded in Mexico City in 1575. Later, Fray Pedro Agurto was named Bishop of Zebú in the Philippines. Another student at Tiripitío was the famous Tarascan leader, Antonio Huitziméngari Caltzontzin, who was a son of the last Tarascan "king." Fray Alonso's work as organizer and teacher at Tiripitío, as a teacher at the University of Mexico City, as founder of the Colegio de San Pablo, and as an author of scholarly books places him high in the ranks of the founders of Mexican culture. His erudition, his energy, and his devotion to the cause of learning, entitle him to be classed with Erasmus as one of the great minds of those times.

The first schools founded for *mestizos* were the Colegio de San Juan de Letrán, for boys, and the Colegio de Nuestra Señora de la Caridad, for girls.[24] It is believed by some that as early as 1529, Fray Pedro de Gante, in connection with the hospital which he founded, had inaugurated the education of *mestizo* boys and girls who had been abandoned by their parents, and that the founding of the above-named schools was carried out

[23] Alegría, *op. cit.*, pp. 215–226.
Zepeda Rincón, *op. cit.*, pp. 55–56, 92–95.   [24] Zepeda Rincón, *op. cit.*, pp. 81–88.

as a continuation and expansion of the services which Fray Pedro had been rendering for *mestizos*. Officially, however, the Colegio de San Juan de Letrán was founded in Mexico City in 1547. This was accomplished largely through the efforts of Archbishop Zumárraga and of Viceroy Mendoza, both of whom had an abiding interest in the welfare of the abandoned *mestizos*. Zumárraga was anxious that similar schools should be established throughout the realm as he recognized the urgent needs inherent in the very nature of this new element of the population. Though at first the curriculum was essentially of an elementary level—reading, writing, doctrine, "good customs," and trades—in a few years the school also served a few students as a normal school and as a preparatory school for the University. This school continued to exist until the first part of the nineteenth century.

It is known that a school for *mestizo* girls existed in Mexico City as early as 1531, for in that year a group of devout women arrived from Spain, and a house, where they gathered abandoned *mestizo* girls, was assigned to them. As suggested before, it is thought that, even before then, Fray Pedro de Gante had been providing the rudiments of an education for some of these girls. In 1548, the Collegio of Nuestra Señora de la Caridad was founded to take over the instruction of *mestizo* girls. In 1552, Spanish girls were permitted to attend the school, the first instance of a school in Mexico opening its doors to them. This school limited itself to instruction in religious doctrine, domestic duties and, on occasion, reading and writing.

It is a source of some astonishment to find that the realistic and liberal views and the widespread interest displayed in the education of Indian boys and girls—best exemplified by Pedro de Gante and Vasco de Quiroga —were not reflected in the education of Spanish and *mestizo* children. Spanish and *mestizo* girls received the same sort of rudiment training that was common for girls in Europe. While this practice might be explainable in the case of Spanish girls considering that they were to live in Mexico much as they would in Spain, that training certainly did not fit the needs of the *mestizo* girls who, without family or social status, were faced with the highly pressing need of a broad and practical education. The education of Spanish boys also followed the European norms—private tutors, convent classes, academic studies, etc. Many were sent to Europe for their education. It is to be regretted that Spanish children did not have their Fray Pedro or "Tata" Vasco to light their way along the new paths of life in the American World—paths strewn with social and economic questions for which the verbalistic education of the Old World had no adequate response.

Though San Juan de Letrán at first sought to emulate Fray Pedro's great Indian school of San José, it soon degenerated and the education of *mestizo* boys along pragmatic lines did not continue to receive the encouragement and support which the realities of the Mexican scene demanded. San Juan de Letrán, nevertheless, continued to exist and to render valuable service until the first part of the nineteenth century.[25] The decline in this school and in the education of *mestizos* in general may be attributed in large part to the death of Archbishop Zumárraga in 1548 and to the fact that Viceroy Mendoza left Mexico in 1550 to become Viceroy of Peru. Thus the *mestizos* lost their two major champions—men who might have saved the *mestizo* from the miserable status into which he was born and from which he was not to rise until more than two centuries later. This does not mean that the doors of learning were closed to the *mestizos,* for they were not excluded from the existing schools. But only the well-to-do among them could aspire to that privilege and the *mestizo* was poor. Besides, the growing masses of *mestizos* needed more than the academic learning offered by existing schools; their condition called for schools of action not of words.

On September 26, 1551, Charles V issued the decree founding the University of Mexico on a plan patterned after that of the University of Salamanca. The decree was issued in response to the repeated requests of many of the leaders in New Spain, among whom Viceroy Mendoza figured prominently. In one of his letters the Viceroy indicates that since about 1539 he had been appointing teachers in all the various faculties who might be carrying on their courses of instruction in anticipation of the founding of the university, and that he had allotted funds for their support. Since, as stated above, Mendoza left Mexico in 1550, he was not in New Spain to officiate at the opening of the institution for which he had labored so assiduously. That privilege fell to his successor, Luís de Velasco. He, after the initial ceremony of January 25, 1553, at which occasion the University was dedicated to Saint Paul (on the anniversary of his conversion), officially inaugurated classes open to all, Spanish, Indians, and *mestizos,* on June 3, 1553, under both the legal and financial patronage of the Spanish Crown. Since the institution also received the sanction of the Pope, then a prerequisite to the conducting of a fully-fledged institution of higher learn-

[25] Castañeda, *op. cit.,* pp. 8–77 ff.

ing in the Catholic world, the institution is properly referred to as the Royal and Pontifical University of Mexico.

The initial curriculum offered courses in theology, the Scriptures, canon law, jurisprudence, the liberal arts, rhetoric, and grammar. It is known that Indian languages, Nahuatl and Otomí, were taught there in its early years, as also later on. In 1582, a course in medicine, that is, of anatomy and physiology was inaugurated. This was expanded in 1595 to include the study of illness (*"cuerpo enfermo"*). Surgery was not introduced until the seventeenth century. The two faculties (or schools) were those of theology and law, and the degrees granted were those of bachelor, licentiate, and master or doctor. By the beginning of the seventeenth century, twenty-three courses had been made available, and, by 1636, when Harvard College was founded, the University of Mexico had graduated more than 8,000 students with the baccalaureate degree.

The significance of the pioneering work of this institution is suggested in the comparison made by Castañeda: [26]

Let us take a glance at the relative progress of education in Mexico and the thirteen English colonies at the beginning of the American Revolution. By 1776, the year of the Declaration of Independence, the Royal and Pontifical University of Mexico had been in continuous operation for two hundred and twenty-three years. During that time it had granted 1,162 doctors' and masters' degrees in all four faculties: Theology, Arts, Canon Law and Civil Law; and it had granted 29,882 bachelors degrees, besides numerous licentiates not recorded. At that time there were in Mexico, in addition to the university, fourteen different colleges or general houses of study of similar rank, many of whose students took graduate courses in the university. Now if we turn to the thirteen American colonies we find that there were nine colleges, not one of which could rightly be called a university. Not until 1779, as a result of the efforts of Thomas Jefferson, was the College of William and Mary, which had been originally granted a charter in 1692 but which did not actually open until 1693, reorganized as a university. The only American colleges founded previous to 1777 were: Harvard, in 1636; William and Mary, in 1693; Yale, in 1701; the College of Philadelphia, now the University of Pennsylvania, in 1749; King's College, now Columbia University, in

26 C. E. Castañeda, "The Beginnings of University Life in America," *Preliminary Studies of the Texas Catholic Historical Association,* Volume III, No. 4, July, 1938, p. 7.

1754; Brown, in 1764; Dartmouth, in 1769; Queen's Rutgers, in 1766; and Hampden-Sidney, in 1776.

The Real y Pontificia Universidad de México continued until 1865, when it was suppressed. Its rebirth in 1910 as the Universidad Nacional de México will be dealt with in the following chapter where its organization and its development from its beginnings in the sixteenth century to the present, will be described.

At various times attempts had been made to attract the Jesuits to New Spain. Soon after the death of Archbishop Zumárraga (1548), the treasurer of the Colegio de San Juan de Letrán, Gregorio Pesquera, sought to interest them in it. In 1553 he went to Spain to try to persuade Ignatius of Loyola to lend his help, but the founder of the Compañía was unable to do so for lack of personnel. In 1561, Martín Cortés, son of the conqueror, who had served a novitiate with the Order, pressed for the sending of Jesuits to found a college of higher studies for which his father had left an endowment. After much delay, the intervention of other influential Jesuits in Spain brought about the signing in 1571, of a royal decree which accorded the needed permission. Dr. Pedro Sánchez, graduate and professor of the University of Alcalá, of which he had formerly been the rector, or also that of the University of Salamanca, was named Provincial for the new undertaking. He and sixteen fellow Jesuits arrived in Mexico City on September 28, 1572, and the great work of the Order begun. Irma Wilson points out that the arrival of the Jesuits was "the high light in the educational achievements of the sixteenth century." [27]

For almost two centuries they practiced their system, emphasizing the classical studies, theatrical representations, literary academies, and public acts. At the time of their expulsion in 1767, they had not only founded more than twenty-five colleges but they had also succeeded in modernizing teaching by the introduction of modern philosophy, and with it the studies of physics and natural history. The early foundations in the city of Mexico, the Colegio de San Pedro y San Pablo (1573), that of San Gregorio (1575), of San Bernardo (1575), and of San Miguel (1576), were intended for the education of the Creoles and were later combined with that of San Ildefonso, with the exception of San Gregorio, which was for the Indians. The Jesuits also directed colleges in Pátzcuaro, Valladolid, Puebla, Oaxaca, Guadalajara, and Vera Cruz.

[27] Wilson, op. cit., pp. 24–25.

As will be noted from the above, the Jesuits were highly active in the establishment of educational institutions in Mexico from the very outset. They not only founded the institutions mentioned above but others as well, both in Mexico City and elsewhere. Many of these schools continued in existence even after the Jesuits were suppressed in the eighteenth century. The Colegio de San Ildefonso, which will be discussed in detail later, has survived to this day. It became the National Preparatory School in 1867 and is now a part of the University of Mexico. In addition, the Jesuits took over the management of institutions that had previously been founded by other orders. The Colegio de San Nicolás Obispo, founded by Bishop Vasco de Quiroga, was among the latter schools. As stated before, this college is still in existence as a part of the University of Michoacán. Like the Colegio de San Ildefonso, the Colegio de San Nicolás will be treated at greater length later. In all these institutions the Jesuits introduced the humanities and their famous plan of teaching—their *ratio studiorum*. Before the coming of the Jesuits to Mexico, higher education in the various colleges and the university was guided by the norms of the medieval universities, by scholasticism. The Jesuits, by introducing the classics of the Greek and Roman civilizations, opened new intellectual horizons to Mexico as they were doing elsewhere in the world. In addition, the Jesuit's plan of study provided for the introduction of realistic studies.

It is not necessary in this study to elaborate upon the pedagogical contributions made by the Compañía de Jesús as those contributions have been reviewed in many texts on the history of education. Beyond a doubt, the Jesuit program in secondary and higher education was a decided improvement upon the traditional practices of that time. The new ideas which that Order introduced into Mexican education constituted a definite step forward in the work of laying the foundations of Mexican culture, a work which had been inaugurated so ably in the institutions founded by other orders and in the University of Mexico. It must be kept in mind, however, that the Jesuit program and method were highly rigid and not susceptible to much change as the years went by. The emphasis placed by the Jesuits on moral and intellectual training, upon the value of classical learning, and upon discipline and loyalty represented a much-needed reform in the education of the early leadership of New Spain. In the sixteenth and seventeenth centuries this emphasis and the tireless efforts of the members of the Order to reach an ever-widening circle of youth cannot be regarded as other than an outstanding contribution. On the other hand, the limitations which Jesuit education placed upon individual initiative and upon adaptation to changing social and economic conditions have represented a most serious deficiency in their plan of work. Since the Jesuit influence dominated higher education in Mexico over a period of two hundred years—a period during which the need for individuality, adaptation, and progressiveness was very great—this limitation constituted a serious obstacle to the development of the Mexican people.

All this is, in effect, to say, that an evaluation of the Jesuit influence in Mexico should be made in terms of the several historical periods involved. The Jesuits rendered an outstanding and liberal service to Mexico when they participated in laying its cultural foundations in the first century of the colony. Later, by perpetuating, largely unchanged, the content of their program and their methods under vastly different circumstances, the Jesuits may be regarded as having handicapped the evolution of the new, the Mexican, culture in the creation of which they had rendered such valuable service.

One of the most remarkable institutions that has ever been established in the Americas was the one established on August 15, 1573, in Mexico City under the name of the "Colegio Mayor de Santa María de Todos Santos." [28] This was an endowed residential center of graduate studies created through the generosity of Dr. Francisco Rodríguez Santos who, out of his private funds, paid for the building and support of the institution which was established to enable ten sons of illustrious families to pursue their higher studies. The significance of this foundation is suggested when it is known that, of the ten "fellows" first named by Dr. Rodríguez Santos, four were post-doctoral students. He stipulated that admission be on the basis of competitive examination and that it be limited to men over twenty years of age on whom the University had bestowed at least a bachelor's degree in either the faculty of theology, law, or canons. As prescribed by the rules of the institution, the students themselves should annually elect one from their membership to be the Rector. Three of the students must be lawyers, three graduates in canons, and four theologians. It was further stipulated that one of them should be a priest, and that he would be Chaplain of the school. Various other regulations, requiring the students to give public lectures, regulations governing their participation in what

[28] Zepeda Rincón, op. cit., pp. 127–130.
Castañeda, op. cit., pp. 26–32.
Castañeda Nuevos Documentos. . . .), pp. 26–32.

we would now call public forums, and matters concerning other phases of the institution were set forth in the rules and by-laws.

This institution continued in operation with varying degrees of success until it was finally closed in 1833. In the course of two hundred and sixty years of service it made itself a residence and study center for such students as the above, and endowed more than three hundred with research fellowships. Many of them bore names that were later to be of high distinction. This is indicated by the list of the first students cited by Zepeda Rincón: [29]

> Sr. D. Juan Orduño Avendaño who was the first Rector of the college, named by Sr. Santos; Sr. Dr. D. Ildefonso Muños Tirado who had been professor of the University of Mexico, Abbot of the Congregation of San Pedro, Priest of Puebla, afterwards Priest-Treasurer and Dean of Mexico, of the Council of His Majesty and Bishop-elect of Chiapa; Sr. Dr. D. Rodrigo Maldanado, later Professor of Canons at the University of Salamanca, Knight of the Order of St. James, of the Council of His Majesty and *oidor* of Granada; Sr. Dr. y Maestro Don José López, who had received his doctorate in Theology and in Canons, who had been on His Majesty's Council and Comptroller of the Audiencia of Guatemala; Sr. D. Gabriel de Mexía, who later was of His Majesty's Council and Comptroller of the Audiencia of Guatemala; Sres. D. Augustín de Coz, Dn. Andrés González de Mendoza and Dr. D. Gonzalo de Alarcón, who had been Arch-Dean of the Church of Guatemala. As may be seen, all the founding students with the exception of two occupied high civil and ecclesiastic positions.

There are indications that in subsequent years the quality of the students of the Colegio de Santa María maintained the same high standards evidenced in this first student body.

The establishment of this endowed institution, with principles so far-reaching as is implicit above, is almost beyond belief. That an individual and a society should place such value upon the highest and finest elements of learning is phenomenal in itself, even had such a concept not been put into practice. That such an idea should be embodied in the establishment of an endowed institution through the highminded philanthropy of an individual living in that period of world history is, to repeat, almost incredible. But this institution became the crowning glory of higher educa-

[29] Zepeda Rincón, *op. cit.,* p. 128.

tion in Mexico in the sixteenth century and it may serve as a fitting symbol for the remarkable attainments of this Golden Age of Mexican history. The vision and the spirit that came together in the Colegio Mayor de Santa María de Todos Santos bring to a culmination the laying of the cultural foundations of Mexico.

It has not been the purpose of this chapter to present an exhaustive description and interpretation of things educational in the sixteenth century. Many schools and colleges which were founded at that time have not been mentioned. Similarly, no reference has been made to the achievements of many distinguished laymen and churchmen. Even far-reaching tendencies, evident during the foundation years, have not been presented or have been given only passing mention. It has been the purpose of this chapter merely to touch upon the great picture which then was higher education in Mexico and not to cover the ground in detail. The glimpses offered into educational endeavor in sixteenth century New Spain make it plain that Mexican educational foundations were, in the large, far ahead of their time and, for their time, highly liberal and progressive. During this period the concepts which presaged the development of a great culture found expression, and the tools essential to its realization were demonstrated. The errors committed and the shortcomings that have been indicated are of small account when compared with the far-reaching assets represented by the genius of the men of those days and the spirit of the institutions which they estáblished. Whatever may be our judgment upon later developments, this was a glorious age in Mexican education. What is more, here in truth is a period to which the modern Mexican educator may go back both for inspiration and for direct guidance in the solution of the formidable problems which face the Mexican nation today.

Chapter Three

FOUR CENTURIES OF HIGHER
EDUCATION

THE CONQUEST and colonization of Mexico embraced such a variety of activities and extended over so great an area that it is difficult to appreciate the full significance of the achievements involved. On the one hand, the techniques of European civilization for the exploitation of resources and for the government of conquered peoples were implanted over wide reaches of territory and among a highly diverse native population. On the other hand, the processes of colonization had to be carried on under the serious handicap of slow and uncertain communications with the mother country and by means of improvised methods and materials in New Spain. The magnitude of these difficulties, even when viewed solely from their material aspects, assume even greater proportions when one realizes that the fundamental achievements in the development of a Mexican culture took place four hundred years ago.

It is noteworthy that the process of organizing colonial life in New Spain was not simply that of establishing the administrative structures that would facilitate the exploitation of resources and the management of the Indians but, as an indispensable and integral phase of this process of organization, the cultural development of the peoples of New Spain became a matter of major concern. This work of cultural development had numerous manifestations. The spread of Christianity alone is worthy of the highest praise and of far greater recognition and study than it has so far been accorded by research workers interested in cultural development in Mexico. The very extensive dissemination of the Spanish language among so many indigenous tribes, who spoke very different languages and were scattered across a wide expanse of forbidding territory, was an outstanding achievement. The administrative organization which, in the course of a few decades after the conquest of Mexico City, reached out to every little town and hamlet from Central America to New Mexico and from Yucatán to California was also an attainment of the highest order. Each in itself offers a major field of study and each has significant implications in Mexico's general cultural development. It is to be noted that these achievements are inescapably related and that the development of education is intimately associated with all of them. It must be borne in mind constantly that the development of Mexican education, both in colonial times and in the present, is but one factor in the total development to which all of these activities contribute.

In the preceding chapter brief mention has been made of New Spain's methods of making use of educational institutions and procedures in this process of total cultural development. That chapter, far from being an exhaustive presentation of even the general contributions made in education during the sixteenth century, is simply a brief introduction to their study. Each of the schools mentioned might well be the subject matter for a volume, and also for both intensive and extensive further research. Many of the educational activities that are known to have then been at work were not even mentioned. The information available on most of the schools of that period is as yet wholly inadequate for a proper evaluation of their accomplishments.

As has already been noted, several of the institutions founded in the sixteenth century persisted through the colonial period and some of them have continued to exist to the present day. The services rendered by these institutions over a period of three or four hundred years are of major import to the present cultural status of the Mexican nation. Though none of the schools ever reached any great part of the Mexican peoples at any one time, the cumulative effect which even the smallest schools exercised through their graduates cannot be over-estimated. From the earliest days of the Conquest and on through the centuries, Mexico has had her group of intellectuals who were constantly striving towards perfection in academic fields, who were constantly impressing themselves upon the social and economic leadership of the times, and who were indefatigably training and guiding groups of students who were to fill places of outstanding importance in their society. Even the most conservative attitude taken by the schools, their faculties, and their students could not but have contributed greatly to the progress of Mexican culture. While, for the purpose of academic study, one may characterize the ideologies and curricula of some of these schools as narrow and conservative, this should not be construed as suggesting that their contribution to the intellectual growth of the colony and the Republic should be discounted. It can be stated categorically that each and all of the institutions already mentioned can be held to constitute a substantial and worthwhile pillar upon which present-day Mexican culture rests. That the schools of the sixteenth century were not able to accomplish more during the colonial regime is due not to the fact that they were sponsored by a conservative church and not because of any intellectual deficiency on the part of their leadership but rather because of the physical and social handicaps imposed by their colonial character and by the material and cultural defects inherent in the field in which they operated. That many of these institutions not only persevered through the centuries but made outstanding contributions in spite of these limitations and defects redounds to their credit and is ample evidence of their worth and of the regard with which they were held.

SAN NICOLÁS OBISPO

The broad significance of the work that Bishop Vasco de Quiroga did in stimulating the cultural development of the common people of the State of Michoacán overshadows the importance of the individual contributions involved in it. Some of these individual contributions, however, even when taken alone, constitute monuments to perpetuate his memory. One of these, the founding of El Colegio de San Nicolás Obispo, represents a noble achievement in the history of Mexican education.

El Colegio de San Nicolás Obispo was founded by Bishop de Quiroga at Pátzcuaro in 1540 for the religious education of both Indians and Spaniards.[1] The school was later transferred to Valladolid (now Morelia) where it has remained to this day. The name of the school was changed to San Nicolás Hidalgo in the nineteenth century in honor of the father of Mexican Independence, Father Miguel Hidalgo y Costilla, who had been pupil, teacher, and rector of the institution. Today the Colegio of San Nicolás is the oldest institution of higher learning in the New World. It is now the preparatory school of the University of Michoacán (Universidad Michoacana de San Nicolás Hidalgo). It has the additional distinction of having been the intellectual cradle of many liberal leaders and movements in Mexico.

When, after having been made Bishop of Michoacán in 1537, Don Vasco was planning the establishment of his cathedral at Pátzcuaro he likewise gave attention to the preparation of priests who would serve in the work of the church in the region which made up his spiritual domain. In this

---

[1] Julián Bonavit, *Historia del Colegio Primitivo y Nacional de San Nicolás de Hidalgo.* Morelia, Departamento de Extensión Universitaria, 1940, p. 341.

connection Juan José Moreno, who wrote Bishop de Quiroga's biography in the latter part of the eighteenth century, has said: [2]

> Our illustrious bishop was so deeply impressed with the indispensable need that a cathedral church has for a college which will be a seminary through which it will be provided with minister for its cult and service that it was one and the same thing to conceive the idea of the cathedral and that of the college.

It is worthy of note, as Moreno also points out, that this thought was a matter of basic consideration with the church leaders who convened at the Council of Trent many years later. With characteristic insight, Bishop de Quiroga anticipated the decisions of that Council and, as Moreno says, it might well be thought that that Council "had no other model for what it decided upon in Chapter 18 of session 23 than that which he had prescribed in Michoacán." The college which he founded under the name of San Nicolás Obispo at Pátzcuaro in 1540 was to be governed by a secular priest and had as its principal object the preparation of those who were to serve the church as priests. Young Spaniards, over twenty years of age, who wanted to dedicate themselves to the study of sacred theology were admitted free. The curriculum, in addition to Latin, included moral theology, canons, and other religious studies. In recognition of the cooperation extended to him by the people of the neighborhood in constructing the college, Bishop de Quiroga provided that they, Indians and mestizos, were also to be admitted free. These latter students were to be taught to read and write "and all else that they wished to learn of what was being taught." [3]

Not only was a way opened for Indian students to enter San Nicolás but special efforts were made by Vasco de Quiroga to see that they took advantage of this opportunity. It was noted in the preceding chapter that the son of the last Tarascan or Caltzontzin king, Don Antonio Huitziméngari Caltzontzin (also known as Antonio Tito Vitziméngari) was a student with Fray Alonso de la Veracruz at the Colegio de Tiripitío. This student taught Fray Alonso the Tarascan language [4] and was regarded as an outstanding scholar in Latin, Hebrew, Greek, Spanish, and the Tarascan language. He also studied at San Nicolás and later became Governor of the Tarascan capital Tzintzunzan. Two other Caltzontzins studied at San Nicolás. One, don Pedro, brother of the last Tarascan king, entered the

2 Aguayo Spencer, *op. cit.,* p. 59.   3 Bonavit, *op. cit.,* p. 7.
4 Teja Zabre, *op. cit.,* p. 187.

novitiate of the Jesuit order and was assigned to duties both in the school and the hospital. He served as a teacher of elementary school subjects at San Nicolás. Both he and the rector of the school (Father Curiel, who will be mentioned later) succumbed to the smallpox epidemic of 1576. Another member of this family, Pablo Caltzontzin, a nephew of the Tarascan king, likewise studied at San Nicolás, and Bonavit states that he is almost sure that he was the first of the Indians to be ordained as a priest of the Christian religion.[5] Historical sources make indirect mention of other Indians who studied at San Nicolás, some of whom taught there or achieved distinction in government or in the Church. Throughout its entire history this school has been a center of training for Indian leaders. Today the rector of the University of Michoacán is a full-blood Tarascan Indian and many of the present and past leaders of the state have been Indians whose training was received at San Nicolás. The tradition set by Bishop de Quiroga has persisted through the centuries, and San Nicolás can be regarded as the cradle of Indian leadership in Mexico, though it should not be overlooked that the Colegio de Santa Cruz de Tlatelolco was founded for the higher education of Indians in 1536, as noted in the preceding chapter.

It is known that Bishop de Quiroga had long hoped to persuade the Society of Jesus to come to New Spain, especially to the Michoacán country.[6] He had written to Ignatius of Loyola and, on Bishop de Quiroga's visit to Spain, had persuaded the founder of the Order to have four of his followers return to New Spain with the Bishop. Unfortunately, at the very moment of departure, they became ill and were unable to make the journey, and thus the coming of the Jesuits to New Spain was delayed until 1572. While the good Bishop was unable to obtain the help of the Jesuits, he continued to stimulate the development of San Nicolás, and numerous students passed through its halls during the balance of his lifetime. After his death in 1565 the school suffered from the lack of his personal stimulation and began to deteriorate in spite of the fact that he had left a large portion of his private holdings to the school for its support, and though he had made adequate provision for the management of the institution by the Council of the Cathedral. As Decorme states in his monumental study on the work of the Jesuits in Mexico, shortly after their arrival in

---

[5] Bonavit, *op. cit.*, p. 18.
See also Aguayo Spencer, *op. cit.*, pp. 61, 150.   [6] Aguayo Spencer, *op. cit.*, pp. 95–97.

1572, the Order was urgently petitioned by the Council to take charge of San Nicolás.[7] He points out that, in 1573, the Order took charge of the school with Father Juan Curiel as Superior of the local Order, and Juan Sánchez was rector at San Nicolás. Sánchez was called to Mexico the very next year and Curiel assumed the rectorship and taught chemistry there. The school immediately began to prosper and, in 1574, it had three hundred students. It is of interest to note that one of the teachers brought in by the Jesuits was Pedro Rodríguez who taught grammar at San Nicolás. He was admitted to the Order while there, and is thought to have been the first of the Jesuits to learn the Tarascan language.

The transfer of the cathedral from Pátzcuaro to Valladolid shortly after the death of Bishop de Quiroga made it necessary that San Nicolás should also go with it. In spite of the objections of the local population, and only after the use of the utmost tact by the Jesuits, San Nicolás was moved to Valladolid in 1580. Since 1531 there had existed near Valladolid a school which had been founded by two Franciscans, Fray Antonio de Lisboa and Fray Juan de San Miguel. This school, El Colegio de San Miguel, was joined with that of San Nicolás in 1581, almost immediately after it had been moved from Pátzcuaro.[8]

The school continued to prosper at Valladolid though there soon developed some dissension over its administration by the Jesuits. This culminated in the withdrawal of the Jesuits from the college late in the sixteenth century. This seems to have been a serious blow to the school, though it continued to operate on a reduced scale for the next eighty years. Little is known in detail of the story of this school during the seventeenth century, though there is a record of reforms instituted in its organization and internal administration in 1675. These reforms lowered the age of admission from twenty years to thirteen or fourteen, and increased the length of the course of studies. During this period, and subsequently, the school had a number of distinguished students and teachers whose names have come down in history.[9]

In 1779, the School of Law was opened through the generosity of Doña

[7] Gerard Decorme, *La Obra de Los Jesuitas Mexicanos Durante La Epoca Colonial 1572–1767.* Mexico. Antigua Librería Robredo de José Porrúa e Hijos, 1941. Volume I, pp. 14–16.

[8] Bonavit, *op. cit.,* pp. 21–36, 42–43.

Jesús Romero Flores, *et al. IV Centenario de Morelia, 1541–1941* (commemorative monograph, publisher unknown), p. 6.

[9] Bonavit, *op. cit.,* pp. 49–61.

Francesa Javiera Villegas y Villanueva, a rich woman who gave a large portion of her wealth to the support of the classes in jurisprudence.[10] By 1810, when San Nicolás was closed because of the War of Independence, the School of Law had graduated fifty-four students—some in civil and some in canon law. It is known that at this time San Nicolás was a flourishing institution. It prepared students for the priesthood, for careers in canon law, and for the profession of civil law. A class in the Tarascan language was open to the students in addition to the usual courses in the professional fields above-mentioned. The War of Independence and subsequent developments kept San Nicolás closed from 1810 to 1847. It was reopened as a state school in 1847 with a course of scientific studies. Among the various courses then offered were Spanish, Latin, chemistry, French, philosophy, mathematics, civil law, and canon law. In 1830 a school of medicine had been opened at Morelia and, in 1847, it became a part of San Nicolás.[11]

From the moment of the reopening of San Nicolás in 1847, the school became a center of liberalism and of modern education. The School of Medicine offered courses for the training of midwives, and soon courses in pharmacy were also being made available. An academy of music was opened in the middle of the nineteenth century and courses in drawing and art likewise found their place in the curriculum of San Nicolás. Modern languages—French, German, Italian and English—were taught, and also commercial courses. Such courses as botany, physics, chemistry, and zoology became an important part of the program of studies and considerable effort was made to develop laboratory facilities. Thus by 1863, when the school was again closed as a result of the French invasion, San Nicolás had become a modern institution of higher learning offering a wide variety of courses which were being constantly adapted to meet the changing conditions of an area that was in the process of adjustment from colonial conditions to that of independence—from the old humanism to the realism of a scientific world.

A school for girls had been founded at Valladolid in the latter part of the seventeenth century. The Colegio de Santa Rosa María was also established for the education of girls in 1757. This school remained in existence until after the middle of the nineteenth century, its program of studies centered upon domestic education, painting, and music.[12] In May, 1886,

[10] *Ibid.*, pp. 95–114.
Macías, *op. cit.*, pp. 129–132, 154–161.
[12] Romero Flores, *et al.*, *op. cit.*, p. 19.

[11] Bonavit, *op. cit.*, pp. 191–225.
Macías, *op. cit.*, pp. 94–117.

there was opened at the Colegio de San Nicolás the Academia de Niñas. It was primarily a normal school, though domestic science, commerce, and the fine arts were taught there also. Later the Academia became the normal school for girls, and in recent years has become a part of the coeducational normal school operating as one of the divisions of the University of Michoacán which has, as its preparatory school and cornerstone, the ancient Colegio de San Nicolás.

In 1882 the first steps were taken towards the creation of a museum which, by 1886, had become a well organized institution. As early as 1888 the museum was publishing the bulletin *Anales del Museo Michoacano* which has been revived in recent years as a scholarly and highly useful research journal. The museum in time came to be a part of the University of Michoacán and has always operated in close association with the Colegio de San Nicolás.

Bonavit and Macías, in the works cited, have dealt in great detail with the development of San Nicolás and its associated institutions from the earliest colonial days to the present. The steady increase in courses and the continuous liberal trend apparent in successive reforms are made very clear. Courses of study were frequently revised and amplified. New fields of intellectual endeavor were constantly being added to the curriculum. All in all, the curricular history of this institution offers the picture of a small school that from its establishment four hundred years ago to the present time has persistently remained in the vanguard of education. The progress observed in the curricular changes made by the school, however, is simply symbolic of the liberally progressive spirit that has always characterized the activities of the faculty and student body of San Nicolás. There has never been a period in the history of this school, from the time of Bishop Vasco de Quiroga to the present day, when its faculty and its students have not been in the front ranks of intellectual and social endeavor in Mexico. The list of its distinguished students and faculty members offers many names which are indelibly etched in the most glorious pages of Mexican history.[13]

Father Miguel Hidalgo y Costilla, the father of Mexican independence, was a student, professor, treasurer, and rector of San Nicolás between the years 1765 and 1792.[14] His distinguished career in that institution and the great impetus that he gave to learning and freedom of thought is one

[13] Bonavit, *op. cit.*, pp. 319–341.
Macías, *op. cit.*, pp. 139–147, 379–3
[14] Universidad Michoacana de San Nicolás de Hidalgo. *Anales del Museo Michoacano*, Morelia, Number 1, July, 1939, pp. 42–57.

of the fondest traditions of the old Colegio de San Nicolás Obispo, which is now called, in honor of this great patriot and intellectual, the Colegio Primitivo y Nacional de San Nicolás de Hidalgo. Among the other great names associated with the student body of San Nicolás are those of José María Morelos y Pavón, the generalissimo of the Mexican War of Independence; Melchor Ocampo Manzano, the great nineteenth century statesman, patriot, and governor of Michoacán; Pascual Ortiz Rubio, ex-president of the Republic; and many other distinguished scientists, educators, and political figures, such, for example, as Dr. Jesús Díaz Barriaga, well known in contemporary medical research, Dr. Enrique Arreguín, Jr., former rector of the University of Michoacán and recently Sub-Secretary of Education, and a host of others who, in colonial days, in the last century, and at the present time have been in the front rank of liberal thought and action in Mexico.

The Revolution of 1910 found many *nicolaitas* [15] among the insurgents, just as they had been prominent leaders in all past national crises—in the War for Independence, the period of Reform, the war with the United States, the struggle with the French invaders, etc. This tradition of independence of thought and action has many times brought down the wrath of conservative authorities upon San Nicolás. In 1895 the School of Medicine was ordered separated from San Nicolás as an punishment for student revolts against the reactionary practices of the state government. For similar reasons the School of Law was made a separate institution in 1901 —leaving San Nicolás, the preparatory school, as the only branch of the once powerful institution which embraced all the major fields of learning and which had a student body united in the pursuit of liberal ideals and progressive social action. This setback to the school, however, did not quell the spirit of revolt among the students and the three schools continued to act as a unified disturbing force opposed to the forces of reaction.[16] Evidence of the manner in which the faculty, students, and graduates of these schools have contributed to intellectual progress is to be found not only in the work that was done within the classrooms and by student organizations but also in activities which were carried on outside the confines of the institution—activities that found expression in newspaper articles, pamphlets, public lectures, literary and artistic societies, scientific study groups, etc.

San Nicolás, like all the other educational institutions of the nation

[15] Alumni of San Nicolás.   [16] Macías, *op. cit.*, pp. 207–234.

underwent a period of virtual abandonment and decay during the Revolution of 1910–17. In 1917 the State Legislature created the Universidad Michoacana de San Nicolás de Hidalgo.[17] The University comprised the old Colegio de San Nicolás, as the preparatory school; the Faculties of Medicine, Jurisprudence, and Engineering; the Museum, the Academy of Fine Arts, the Industrial School for Girls, the two normal schools, and the Industrial School for Boys. Shortly afterwards there were added the Commercial School, the public library of the state, the biological laboratory, and the meteorological observatory. The charter of 1917 creating the University was broadened in 1933, and gave the several schools greater authority in the administration of the institution. The charter was again broadened in 1939, and both student body and faculty were given still greater participation in the management of the school. In addition, the University was assigned responsibilities consonant with the socialistic tendencies of revolutionary Mexico.[18]

Probably one of the outstanding characteristics of San Nicolás, both in its past and recent history, is to be observed in the degree to which democratic principles have been practiced in its administration. From the very beginning, Bishop de Quiroga provided that the student body should have a voice in the administration of the affairs of the school. The regulations which he established for the management of the institution gave it a degree of independence which kept it free from undesirable control by vested interests. This independence was not only maintained in later reforms—those of the latter part of the seventeenth century, of 1847, 1867, 1883, 1917, 1933, and 1939—but academic freedom and liberty of action for both student body and faculty were progressively safeguarded. While this freedom has sometimes been abused it has, in the long run, served well the purpose of progress and intellectual development. Furthermore, this tradition of intellectual freedom and administrative independence has become a highly prized heritage. The graduates of the institution are associated in societies which glory in this heritage and which seek to carry out in public life the principles which were instilled in them as students at San Nicolás. That heritage has served as a dominant force in the cultural development of

[17] Macías, *op. cit.,* pp. 323–348.

[18] *Ibid.,* pp. 349–79.

See also: *Universidad Michoacana,* Bulletin of the University of Michoacán, Morelia, July, 1939, pp. 3–27.

Hacia La Reforma Universitaria. Publication of the University of Michoacán, Morelia, 1939, 84 pp.

Mexico and may be considered as the soundest criterion for determining what is and what is not autonomy in higher education in Mexico. It is one thing to bestow autonomy upon an institution through legislation or other governmental action; it is still another to practice intellectual and academic freedom and autonomy. The autonomy of El Colegio de San Nicolás and of the University of Michoacán has not been due simply to legislative decree. It has always been a real and vital force in the life of this institution. The legal autonomy which the school has attained in recent years has been an earned autonomy and one which, in the light of past contributions of the students and faculty of this institution, is richly deserved. In more than four hundred years of service, El Colegio de San Nicolás de Hidalgo, to-day the oldest institution of higher learning in the New World, has attained distinction not only because of its ancient lineage but also because it has consistently and courageously pioneered the intellectual, the social, and the economic frontiers of its society.

THE UNIVERSITY OF MEXICO

In order to serve God and the public welfare of our kingdoms, it is convenient that our vassals and natural subjects have therein universities and centers of general studies where they may be instructed in all the sciences and faculties. We, therefore, because of our great love and our desire to favor and honor those who live in our Indies, and in order to banish the darkness of ignorance from there forever, hereby create, establish, and order to be founded in the city of Lima, of the Kingdom of Peru, and in the city of Mexico, of New Spain, a university or center of general studies in each respectively, and it is our will to grant to all those persons that may be graduated in the said universities the enjoyment of all privileges and exemptions in our Indies, Islands, and Tierra Firme de Mar Oceano, now enjoyed by those who are graduated by the University of Salamanca.[19]

The keystone of higher education in Mexico has been the school founded by the royal decree of 1551, which was opened in 1553 as the Royal and Pontifical University of Mexico. This school, which disputes with the University of San Marcos in Lima, Peru, the distinction of being the oldest university in the New World, has served as the basic institution of higher learning in Mexico for almost four hundred years. Its influence upon its in-

[19] Quoted from Castañeda, *op. cit.* (The Beginnings of University Life. . . .), p. 14.

tellectual development cannot be over-estimated. From the very beginning distinguished men of letters have served on its faculty. The cream of the youth of Mexico has passed through its halls preparatory to service in Church and State, in business, and in science and letters. Whereas San Nicolás is a shining example of liberalism and of a militant spirit of social reform, the University of Mexico has achieved greatness because of its scholarship and of the mantle of intellectual dignity which it has worn so well from its very inception as the capstone of intellectual endeavor in sixteenth-century New Spain.

It has already been noted that the leaders of New Spain had begun to seek the establishment of a university very soon after the conquest of Mexico. Archbishop Zumárraga, Viceroy de Mendoza, and others often petitioned for such an institution. There is some evidence that suggests that Antonio de Mendoza, had, with his own funds, been financing a university faculty as early as 1539.[20] Some students of the question think that, when the university was opened some fourteen years later, that opening was but a continuation of these earlier faculties and was, in effect, the official confirmation of an accomplished act.

The faculty of the University was composed of distinguished scholars of New Spain. Fray Alonso de la Veracruz was professor of Scholastic Theology; Francisco Cervantes de Salazar, a distinguished Spanish author and university professor, held the chair of rhetoric, and so on through a list of names of men who represented the leading universities of Europe and who had attained reputations in Europe or New Spain both as teachers and as scholars.[21] The first rector of the University was the *oidor* Don Antonio Rodríguez de Quesada, assisted by another *oidor,* Gómez de Santillana as *maestre-escuelas.*[22]

The University was organized after the pattern of medieval universities as represented by that of Salamanca. The program of studies was essentially scholastic—the method of instruction centering on the presentation of problems, and discussion according to the established rules of the scholastic method. In Chapter II mention has been made of the subjects of study offered and the number of students concerned. In spite of the restrictive nature of the scholasticism which governed the functioning of the Uni-

[20] *Ibid.,* p. 10.   [21] *Ibid.,* pp. 15–20.

[22] The *maestre-escuelas* was the chancellor of studies who served as dean and censor. He was considered a direct representative of the King and the Pope, and was the only person authorized to grant degrees. The granting of degrees was not only an academic event but a religious ceremony as well.

versity and which characterized its methodology, the school performed valuable services as a center of higher learning.[23] Though the University underwent various reforms between its founding and 1645, these reforms were not directed towards changing the verbalistic and scholastic character of the institution, and the school continued to function under its medieval cloak through the seventeenth, eighteenth, and part of the nineteenth centuries. While the Jesuits were engaged in introducing humanistic learning and some realistic studies into the curricula of their higher schools, the University of Mexico continued to remain averse to the new fields of study and to perpetuate the outmoded norms of a by-gone age.

As Dr. Alfonso Pruneda states in his introduction to the 1940 *Anuario* of the University, "The decadence of the University became more and more pronounced." As the years went by, in contrast with other institutions of higher learning in the nation which were seeking to respond to newer trends of learning, it continued to follow narrow scholastic standards. Even the War of Independence failed to shake its indifference to new educational trends. It is not surprising, then, that the educational reformers of the early nineteenth century should feel that the University had outlived its usefulness, that it was "useless, unreformable and pernicious," and decided that "it was necessary to suppress it." [24]

On October 19, 1835, it was suppressed and its functions were assigned to six separate schools: a preparatory school, a school of humanities, a school of physical and mathematical sciences, a school of medicine, one of jurisprudence, and one of ecclesiastical sciences. However, before the organization of these schools could be perfected, another decree, that of 1834, re-established it. This re-establishment, however, was not enough to give it new life. It continued as a moribund center of learning until 1856 when it was again suppressed, to be reopened once more in 1856 and suppressed again in 1861. The French occupation brought the school halfway back to life. But finally, in 1865, Maximilian decreed its final suppression.

To all intents and purposes, indeed the University of Mexico had ceased to function as an important center of higher studies in 1810, with the beginning of the War of Independence. From 1821 to 1865 the institution was a university in name only and, during its intermittent periods of official

[23] See: Zepeda Rincón, *op. cit.,* pp. 99–116.

[24] Universidad Nacional Autonoma de México, *Anuario 1940.* Preface by Dr. Alfonso Pruneda, pp. 3–8. (These *Anuarios* are issued for each school or faculty. In addition to giving a summarized history of the university and of the particular school, the laws governing the university and the program of studies of the given school are presented in detail.)

existence, did little more than confer poorly earned titles and degrees which in no way compared with those of the past. Since the university represented the conservative forces and was closely aligned with the clergy, it became a bone of contention between liberals and conservatives. Again to quote Dr. de Pruneda on page 5 of the *Anuario* already cited,

> During those years, the conservative or reactionary governments sought to maintain it for what it signified ideologically; whereas liberal and reform governments made every effort to do away with it because in no way did it correspond to national educational exigencies and because it had come to be the symbol of reactionary ideas.

While the liberal leaders of the latter part of the nineteenth century were bitterly opposed to the principles for which the ancient university had stood, they recognized nevertheless the need for a national center of higher studies. Gradually there developed a sentiment which sought the establishment of such an institution. Finally, through the efforts of Justo Sierra, the distinguished educator and Minister of Public Instruction and Fine Arts, President Díaz asked Congress to take steps to that end. The law creating the National University of Mexico was approved on May 24, 1910, and the school was solemnly inaugurated on September 22. At the opening ceremonies Justo Sierra said,[25]

> The University has no history; the Pontifical University is not the antecedent, it is the past; the new University desires to base itself fundamentally on scientific investigation; its educative action must result from its scientific functioning under the leadership of chosen groups of Mexican intellectuals who desire to cultivate the pure love of truth, and who must persevere day by day and determinedly to see to it that truth, the tests of science, and the interest of the fatherland must be united in the soul of every Mexican in order to create a type of character destined to crown the great task of popular education . . . He who has had a college training must not limit his thinking to himself alone. It should be impossible for us ever to forget either humanity or fatherland . . .

With guiding principles such as these, expressed by the leading thinkers of the period, the National University of Mexico came into being charged with the task of serving as a guiding institution of higher learning for national education. The University was made up of existing schools: the

[25] *Ibid.*, pp. 5–6.

National Preparatory School, the School of Jurisprudence, the Schools of Medicine, Engineering, Fine Arts, and a newly created National School of Higher Studies. The university was made a dependency of the Secretariat of Public Instruction and Fine Arts under the immediate administration of a rector appointed by the President of the Republic. The internal governing council was made up of representatives from the faculty and student body and from the Secretariat of Education. At various times other departments and schools were added to the University and several institutes were formed within the faculty.

During these formative years the new University began to incline towards independence of the national government. Various groups of students and faculty members began to make proposals that it be granted autonomy; and, by the law of July 10, 1929, it became an autonomous institution with its own internal system of government. Within that system the several faculties and schools, their teaching personnel and student bodies, as well as other divisions of the University, were to constitute the electorate. The rector would be selected by the University Council from a list of names nominated by the President of the Republic. The National Government was to continue to subsidize the institution. This was an important forward step towards securing autonomy for the university. Nevertheless, there were elements that were not satisfied with these gains but wished to have complete autonomy. This was the source of various disturbances and considerable agitation went on among both members of the faculty and the student body. As a result, the National Congress finally passed a law, on October 19, 1933, which gave the University complete autonomy. This law has continued in effect to the present day.[26] It makes the University a private institution which has as its ends the development of higher education and the promotion of scientific study, particularly as they are concerned with national problems and conditions, in order that the University may produce professional men and specialists of value to society and helpful in the development of an all-round culture. Under the law, the Federal Government agreed annually to put at the disposal of the University the sum of $10,000,000 (pesos). In 1941–42 the federal subsidy amounted to $3,000,000 (pesos).

The original faculties of the Royal and Pontifical University of Mexico

---

26 See: Universidad Nacional Autónoma de México, *Estatuto General De La. . . .* Mexico, Imprenta de la Universidad, 1939.

These statutes, and the regulations and by-laws of the university, are reproduced in each of the *Anuarios* previously cited.

had been those of Theology and Jurisprudence. Towards the latter part of the sixteenth century courses in Medicine had been added and these, in time, had been expanded to constitute the Faculty of Medicine. These three faculties continued to be the major fields of university study throughout the rest of the colonial period. In the several reorganizations attempted in the nineteenth century prior to the final suppression of the University, reference was made to new departments in the field of the humanities and the sciences. However, the medieval tradition of the institution was not amenable to the development of these new fields and, in the main, the curriculum and the methodology of the school continued to be characterized by scholasticism. It was not until long after the new National University was founded in 1910 that these subjects assumed importance. As will be noted later, the Faculty of Philosophy and Letters was established in 1925 and the Faculty of Sciences in 1938.

The School of Law is the oldest of the schools or faculties of the University, since it has had a continuous existence from the time of the opening of the University in 1553—and probably from an earlier date, as suggested above—until the present time. This school, as well as the School of Medicine, underwent numerous reforms during the nineteenth century —changes in curricula, locale and administration. Whenever the University was suppressed, these schools became independent institutions, sometimes associated with other existing colleges. The School of Medicine, for example, was made a part of the Colegio de San Ildefonso in 1843. One should emphasize the fact, too, that, while the University was suppressed in 1865 and remained closed until 1910, the component parts of the institution continued to function as separate schools. That is to say that, while the administrative structure which united the schools as a university was outlawed, the higher education offered by the schools which composed the University was still available. The schools of Law and Medicine have continued to be the most important of the higher schools in Mexico. Reference to the table presented on pages 104–105 brings this out very clearly. Of 685 degrees granted by the University in 1940, 518 were granted by the Faculties of Law and Medicine.

The School of Medicine, inaugurated in 1582 in the course offered by Dr. Juan de la Fuente, developed slowly through the years.[27] Surgery and Anatomy were introduced in the early part of the seventeenth century. The

---

[27] Universidad Nacional Autónoma de México. *Anuario de la Facultad de Medicina 1940.* Mexico, 1939, pp. 53–73.

courses in medicine were, as was common in medieval universities, verbalistic and non-laboratory. It was a long time before surgery was taught by surgeons and it was not until Charles III established the Royal School of Surgery through the decree of 1768 that the beginnings of practical training were made. Though the founding of this royal college gave some impetus to laboratory activities and to hospital practice, the teaching of medicine still was highly academic and the professional career continued to be very badly organized. When the University was closed in 1833 various organizations sought to carry on medical education. Out of these there became by 1843 what was known as the School of Medicine. At that time it was associated with El Colegio de San Ildefonso. In 1847 it was transferred to the building formerly occupied by El Colegio de San Juan de Letrán. Finally, in 1854, it moved to the buildings which had housed the Inquisition and there it has remained to this day. The School of Medicine has slowly expanded its program of studies and has gradually introduced scientific methods.

When the University was re-established in 1910, one of its constituent parts was a newly created graduate school—the Escuela Nacional de Altos Estudios. It was intended that this school should offer graduate study in philosophy and letters and the sciences. Its creation was due to the recognition that in the past the University had leaned too markedly towards the medieval pattern and was sadly in need of these new courses. However, the new school had no recognized plan of studies and offered only a few isolated courses of general cultural value which appealed largely to secondary school teachers. The science courses were in no way suitable to the preparation of specialists and laboratory facilities were almost entirely lacking.[28] Reyes, on pages 53 and 54 of the reference above, has characterized the venture thus:

> The foundation of the new National University . . . seems not to have been sufficiently well-prepared on the administrative side. Actually, what was founded was a coordinated council among already existing and diverse faculties. The new School, that of Higher Studies, though it had a management and a locale, existed most largely on paper. It did not offer a defined program, it did not have its own faculty. The School of Higher Studies did not reveal to the public the ends which it was to fill. It did not offer educational plans, it did not organize careers. The only pro-

[28] Alfonso Reyes. *Pasado Inmediato y Otros Ensayos*. Mexico, El Colegio de México, 1941, pp. 53–64.

fessors on its rolls were three of foreign birth; two of them, Baldwin and Boas, were of high repute distinguished in contemporary science, the other (Reiche) a very able American botanist; mention was made of the coming of others equally famous in the near future . . . The fall of the old regime came about and the School, ignored by the government, orphaned as regarded any defined program, began to live an unfortunate life and be the chosen victim of attacks by those who do not understand . . .

In 1925 the Escuela de Altos Estudios became the Faculty of Philosophy and Letters, while the sciences still remained a poor relation in higher education. Gradually, the science courses were organized into sections of the faculty and, after numerous changes during which the various departments of science were shifted back and forth among the several schools and faculties, the School of Physical and Mathematical Sciences was organized in 1937. The next year this school was converted into the Faculty of Sciences. These numerous changes had not only handicapped scientific study but given evidence of a serious administrative uncertainty as to the place of sciences and of scientific research in the program of higher education.

The Faculty of Sciences is now composed of seven departments: Mathematics, Physics, Chemistry, Biology, Geology, Geography, and Astronomy. The Faculty offers the degrees of Master of Sciences and Doctor of Sciences as well as the titles of Geologist and of Professor of Mathematics, Physics, and Geography. The latter are intended for those who are to teach in secondary and preparatory schools. The Faculty of Philosophy and Letters is divided into the sections of Philosophy, Psychology, Letters, History, Cultural Anthropology, and Educational Sciences. It offers the degrees of Master of Philosophy, Master of Letters, Doctor of Philosophy, and Doctor of Letters. To those who have one of the above degrees, the Faculty offers a program of studies leading to the degrees of Master of Educational Sciences and Doctor of Educational Sciences. These two new Faculties, as well as those of Engineering and Chemical Sciences, and that of Fine Arts, have not yet attained maturity within the University. The great majority of students still flock to the traditional schools of Law and Medicine. The courses offered serve largely as electives to students who are not seeking a degree or who are studying law or medicine.

SAN ILDEFONSO AND THE NATIONAL
PREPARATORY SCHOOL

The first of the schools founded by the Jesuits in New Spain was the Colegio de San Pedro y San Pablo which was opened in Mexico City in 1573, one year after the arrival of the first Provincial, Dr. Pedro Sánchez and sixteen other members of the Order.[29] The Provincial himself acted as the first rector of this school though, at the end of a month, he named Licenciado Gerónimo López Ponce for that position. The new school and its teachers were enthusiastically received. The humanistic curriculum and the advanced pedagogical norms introduced by the Jesuits were a refreshing change from the lugubrious and mystical standards of the scholasticism which prevailed elsewhere. San Pedro y San Pablo could not accommodate all the students who wished to attend, so, in 1575 and 1576, three other similar schools were opened—San Bernardo, San Miguel, and San Gregorio.

There is some doubt as to whether the Colegio de San Ildefonso originated as a separate school at this same time or was simply a new name by which several of the above named schools were known when they were joined in 1588, or in 1567 or 1583, according to some authorities.[30] It is known that by 1612–1618 all the above named institutions formed one school called the Colegio Real de San Pedro y San Pablo y San Ildefonso. San Gregorio was founded for Indian boys through the aid given Dr. Sánchez by the Indian chief of Tacuba who, it seems, was concerned over the decay of the Colegio de Santa Cruz de Tlatelolco and was anxious to have the Jesuits revive Indian education. While this school became a part of San Ildefonso, as indicated above, another institution by the same name and for the same purpose was opened later. This latter institution was organized as a continuation of San Gregorio and became a charitable institution for the education of Indian boys. With the fund donated by a prominent citizen in 1683 it obtained a new lease on life and was able to function until the nineteenth century.

From the time of its organization in the last quarter of the sixteenth century until 1767, when the Jesuit Order was expelled from New Spain, San Ildefonso was a great center of higher education. In contrast with the

[29] Zepeda Rincón, *op. cit.*, pp. 119–122.
[30] Castañeda (*Nuevos Documentos. . . .*), pp. 1–71.
Decorme, *op. cit.*, I, 3–28.
Zepeda Rincón, *op. cit.*, pp. 119–120.

narrow academic tendencies which characterized the Royal and Pontifical University of Mexico, San Ildefonso was a brilliant example of the relatively liberal curriculum sponsored by the Jesuits. Studies centered upon Latin grammar, philosophy, theology, canon law, and the humanities. The Jesuits' plan of studies and their well-ordered methods gave the students an education in which mild discipline, academic awards, public presentations, the drama and literary clubs formed an essential part of the program. Latin, Greek, Spanish, and, at times, Nahuatl were studied and played a part in public speeches, dramas, pageants, etc. Realistic studies such as physics, natural history, and mathematics had their place in the curriculum alongside the study of the classics.

Under the stimulation of this liberal program, San Ildefonso prospered for two hundred years. However, this very liberalism in education was one of the points of conflict which brought about the suppression of the Jesuit Order in 1767. From that date on, the school's outlook was dominated more and more by the restricted criteria of the conservative forces which cared little for the humanism of the Jesuits or for the realistic studies which they had included in their educational plan. At a time when experimentation and the scientific method, when the natural and exact sciences were beginning to achieve a basic place in the schools of northern Europe, Mexico tended to revert to scholasticism, to verbalistic studies, and to prescribed texts and points of view. Though the Jesuits were reinstated for a brief period in the early part of the nineteenth century (1816–1821), from 1767 on San Ildefonso deteriorated rapidly until it was finally closed in 1865. In spite of several attempts to reform this school, both before and after the War of Independence, San Ildefonso continued to hold to the sterile standards of the last days of the eighteenth century. As during that time and previously the school had been closely associated with the University, San Ildefonso was closed in 1865 for much the same reasons which motivated the closing of the University that same year.

The triumph of Benito Juárez over the French was also the triumph of liberal thought over that of the conservative groups which looked back to the colonial times and to scholastic norms for their inspiration. The new regime immediately took steps to reform education along liberal lines. The Minister of Justice and Public Instruction, Antonio Martínez de Castro, charged Francisco Díaz Covarrubias with the task of planning such reforms along broad lines. Covarrubias, in turn, called upon Gabino Barreda to organize the National Preparatory School. Thus, in 1867, San

Ildefonso was transformed and became the cornerstone of modern higher education in Mexico.

Barreda [31] gave the natural and exact sciences a prominent place in the curriculum and he stressed the scientific method as being the fundamental procedure in study. His plan called for an encyclopaedic education in which the verbalism of the humanities would be balanced by the objectivity of the sciences. It is doubtful if many understood the educational philosophy back of Barreda's innovations. His program was soon made the target of many attacks and the school gradually was forced to give way to crippling changes. Some opposed the liberal humanism and philosophy of his course of study. Others objected both to science courses and to scientific methods. Finally, in 1878, Gabino Barreda was sent as minister to Germany and the school was left without a champion for the well-balanced classical and scientific curriculum which he had sought to implant as one which would prepare Mexican students for leadership in the modern world. Even Barreda's followers did not penetrate to the heart of his educational ideas for, in combating attacks upon the sciences, they went to the extreme of undermining the humanities. By 1910 the school was following the highly formal and academic program in which both the sciences and the humanities had degenerated to verbalism and learning by rote. The school which Gabino Barreda had envisioned as a force to regenerate intellectual life in Mexico along modern lines had, forty-three years after its founding, become spiritless and unrealistic.

The National Preparatory School became a part of the National University of Mexico in 1910 and its program of studies was revised. Since then, the school has formed a part of the University although, prior to the passage of the law granting autonomy to the University, the National Preparatory School had come under the jurisdiction of dependencies of the Secretariat of Education and, during the period 1917–21 when the Secretariat did not exist, it functioned under the authority of the Federal District. The re-establishment of the Secretariat in 1921, with José Vasconcelos at its head, gave new impetus to education in Mexico. However, by this time, the National Preparatory School was thought of almost exclusively as merely a collegiate preparatory institution. Its curriculum did not design to prepare students along broad scientific, social, and humanistic lines. It concerned itself only with subjects which were regarded as prerequisite for the careers to be followed in one of the faculties or schools of the Uni-

[31] See the next chapter for a further discussion of Barreda and the Preparatory School.

versity. The Secretariat of Education recognized this restriction on secondary education and, in 1927, limited the preparatory school to the upper two years of its program, and made the first three years a part of the national program of secondary education, or *segunda enseñanza*.[32] The National Preparatory School is today a preparatory school giving a two-year course, and constitutes one of the component parts of the National Autonomous University of Mexico.

[32] See footnote on page 89.

Chapter Four

HIGHER EDUCATION TODAY

A RECENT HERITAGE AND SOME SALIENT FEATURES

THE REVOLUTION which took place in Mexico during the second decade of the twentieth century marked off the old from the new in Mexican education. Those ten years of virtually anarchic strife and devastation constituted a pivotal period in Mexican development, a period during which all the social and economic processes of the nation took a new direction and a new tempo. These historical changes became both the motivating force and the justification for a cultural reconstruction, which is still under way today and which permeates every phase of Mexican life. The Revolution gave a new outlook to Mexican education, an outlook which veered away from the traditional limitations inherited from the colonial order and from the tentative and uncoordinated attempts of a century of independence.

The Mexican Revolution was a spectacular uprising of the Mexican masses and, in the large, it represented an uncompromising break with the social and economic norms of the past. However, the process of changing from the old to the new in social institutions is a complex one and one which cannot be carried out overnight. The heritage of the past is a part of the entire life of a nation and is deeply rooted in modes of thought, and procedures of action, as well as in the structure of institutions. Even a far-reaching revolution does not wipe the slate of society clean. The cultural development of a people does not make a sudden right- or left-hand, ninety-degree turn in the short space of a decade. Both the credits and the debits of the past project themselves into the process of change, influencing its direction, conditioning its scope, and determining its rapidity.

The changes which have been taking place in Mexican education since 1920 are no exception to this general rule of cultural development and they must be studied both in the light of the goals set by the Revolution and in the light of how far the viewpoints and practices of the past have injected themselves into recent reforms. Though these reforms are ostensibly intended to be a break with a progress-stilling tradition, they retain some of the elements which were characteristic of the educational standards of a way of life that post-Revolution Mexico disavows. Again, this is understandable, for education is a social enterprise which cannot be inaugurated *de novo* but which leans heavily on the past. It is this projection of old viewpoints and standards into the educational products of the Revolution that lies at the root of some of the major educational problems of today. The conflict between what might be regarded as the Leftist educational goals of the Revolution and the Rightist inherited educational tools and standards with which the new schools must be constructed represents the most serious issue confronting public education in Mexico today. The very success of the liberal educational goals envisioned by the Revolution will be determined in large part by the degree to which the tools and standards inherited from a conservative past are adapted to present-day ends and by the extent to which new instruments and methods, suited to the development of the modern programs, are created or acquired.

The humanistic refinements of the old colleges, which characterized even the work done in such fields as mathematics and physics, were wholly inadequate to meet the problems which faced the Republic in such fields as those of engineering, public health, exploitation of resources, industrialization, and political organization and administration. It was early recognized that the crux of this deficiency was to be found in the ignorance of the masses. Elsewhere [1] we have shown how the thinkers of the revolutionary movement sought to overcome this intellectual mass inertia. The Constitution of 1917 gave a new meaning to popular education and made the school an instrument of social reform. During recent years, Mexico has attracted widespread attention as a result of its efforts to inaugurate a national program of mass education. These efforts, as represented by the remarkable achievements in rural and Indian education as well as by the general reorganization and expansion of urban education, have revealed a promising creativeness in the development of elementary, secondary, and teacher education in Mexico.

The progress made in the extension of educational opportunity to the masses since 1921 has been a matter of astonishment to the world at large. The founding of kindergartens, of adult classes, of rural schools, and of a multitude of other centers of popular instruction has gone on apace and reached the point where, in the course of a score of years, Mexico has laid the basic groundwork for an enlightened people. [2] In 1906 there were less

[1] Sánchez (*Mexico—A Revolution by Education*).
[2] Goodwin Watson, "Education and Social Welfare in Mexico." A report, The Council for Pan American Democracy, January, 1940, p. 47.

than 800,000 pupils in all public and private schools in Mexico,[3] or less than 5 per cent of the country's population. Some 85 per cent of the people were illiterate. In 1941 there were 23,191 schools. They had a total enrollment of 2,038,000 students, who were being instructed by 47,000 teachers.[4] These figures indicate that the percentage of the total population enrolled in schools has more than doubled since 1906. When it is realized that this growth has taken place almost entirely since 1920, the progress made becomes even more impressive. While no exact figures on the reduction of the illiteracy ratio are available, it is generally estimated that that ratio is now less than 40 per cent.

Numerous works, by both foreign and Mexican students, have set forth the achievements of the Revolution in the field of popular education, and widespread attention has been focused upon those achievements. Elsewhere, the present writer could say this: [5]

It has not been long since Mexico inaugurated its spectacular program of mass education. That program, seeking the redemption of the Mexican masses through a realistic adaptation of education to the demands of the Mexican scene, spread over the nation and attained unprecedented results. The rural teacher, the Cultural Mission, the Indian school, reached out militantly to unshackle the Mexican from the fetters of ignorance and filth, of hunger and oppression. In twenty short years, the revolutionary administration of the nation did a remarkable job of channeling the expression of nationalism along Mexican ways, in the interests of Mexicans, and for the enhancement of Mexican culture. The schools of the Republic attracted the admiration of the world by their intelligent application of principles of acculturation and by the fervor and determination with which they dedicated themselves to the task of "cultivating culture" at the grass-roots of the nation.

The development of popular education is best illustrated by statistics.[6] Between the years 1931 and 1937 the number of primary rural schools under federal support increased from 6,100 to over 11,000, the number of teachers increasing from 7,500 to 15,000, while the enrollment of pupils rose from

[3] Gruening, op. cit., p. 515.

[4] Secretaría de Educación Pública. Memoria, 1940–1941. Mexico. 1941, p. 13.

[5] George I. Sánchez, "Educational Crisis in Mexico," Butrava, Annual Bulletin of The Bureau of University Travel, No. 6, February, 1942, p. 4.

See also: George I. Sánchez, "Education," Mexico Today, the Annals of the American Academy of Political and Social Science, Vol. 208, March, 1940, pp. 144–152.

[6] See: The Memorias of the Secretaría de Educación Pública; also Watson, op. cit.

467,000 to 783,000. Between the same years the number of kindergartens rose from 86 to 319, the number of teachers increasing from 269 to 580. In 1937 the kindergartens enrolled almost 29,000 children whereas the enrollment in 1931 had been only a little over 11,000. It is significant to note that elementary education has now become a function primarily of the Federal Government. More than one million of the 1,388,000 pupils enrolled in primary schools are in federal schools. In this connection it is important to note that federal expenditures for education, which amounted to some 8,000,000 pesos in 1910, had grown to 71,000,000 pesos in 1938 and in 1941 were increased to 91,000,000 pesos. The full import of these increases is not fully appreciated unless it is realized that these amounts refer only to the expenditures of the National Secretariat of Public Education. As indicated by the quotation below, at present these are not the only public expenditures for education: [7]

> The budget assigned to the Secretaría of Educación Pública during the fiscal year (1940–41) reached the amount of (in pesos) $77,850,000 or 15.79 per cent of the grand total of the general budget of expenditures by the Federation. Furthermore, that allocation was also augmented in the course of the year by $326,275.98. If we add to these sums the $12,000,000 the approximate sum spent by the Secretarías of Asistencia Pública, Agricultura, Defensa-Nacional, and Departamentos Central, Salubridad, and Asuntos Indígenas in educational fields, the grand total spent by the Federal Government for public education reached the sum of $90,176,275.98 —a sum which, joined to the $45,056,958 spent by the government of the states and territories, adds up to $135,233,230.98, devoted to education in the entire Republic.

THE HERITAGE OF THE CENTENARY [8]

Prior to 1910 education in Mexico was colonial and aristocratic in character. As has been pointed out in the preceding chapter, the humanistic tradition established during the seventeenth and eighteenth centuries and the selective and exclusive scope of all institutions of learning persisted throughout the nineteenth century in spite of the liberal tendencies of independent Mexico. As has been stated before, in 1906 less than 5 per cent of the population was in school and 85 per cent of the people were illiterate.

[7] Secretaría de Educación Pública. *Memoria, 1940–1941*, p. 19.
[8] The one-hundredth anniversary of the beginning of the War of Independence.

These figures reveal that, in spite of the widespread interest in education evinced during the nineteenth century, and even though many efforts were made to modernize the schools, fundamentally little had been accomplished towards the creation of a nation-wide system of schools. No matter how forward-looking the theory of education in the nineteenth century or how modern and progressive certain schools established may have been, the fact remains that educational opportunity was restricted to the select few and that the schools cannot be regarded as having attained importance as social institutions charged with national cultural rehabilitation. In summarizing educational development for the first fifteen years after the winning of independence, Evelyn Blair says: [9]

Failure to achieve a truly democratic government in Mexico has without doubt been due chiefly to failure of early plans for the education of the people. It is evident that plans for education failed because of financial straits, indecision as to responsibility for education, and lack of conviction on the part of the privileged classes as to the necessity for schools. On the other hand, the failure of schools may be considered a failure of government. Cause and effect are here too closely related to permit of differentiation.

Easy as it is, however, to point out Mexico's backwardness in educational matters, it is evident that there was a genuine and intelligent interest in education between 1821 and 1836. This interest manifested itself in spite of political disturbances, poverty, and unfamiliar responsibilities. Most of the activity took place in the centers of population, and there was little or no education in rural localities. Even the agricultural schools which were projected or attempted had an urban setting. Tangible results were not extensive; lasting achievements were practically nil; but the movements which did take place were not unimportant and were, moreover, a necessary prelude to later progress. Indubitably, the thought and action of this brief era respecting education foreshadowed subsequent history. Throughout this period can be traced the persistence of the idea first introduced into Mexico: a program of Indian education, activity schools, and a form of culture close to the lives of the people. This program, long dormant after the time of Pedro de Gante, had been revitalized by the work of Father Hidalgo, and was to gather

---

[9] Evelyn Blair, "Educational Movements in Mexico, 1821–1836," unpublished doctoral dissertation, The University of Texas, 1941, pp. 322–324.

strength all during the regime of Benito Juárez. By preserving the ideal of sixteenth century educators, the efforts of the early national period helped create the slogan of the present Mexican program: *To educate is to redeem.*

The last decades of the nineteenth century did see the establishment of a basis upon which to found a system of public education. The main outlines of an educational system were laid down, and a few elementary and secondary schools were established here and there under the Republic, primarily in the larger cities and towns. Most of these schools were motivated by liberal views which sought to break away from the rudimentary and verbalistic pattern of colonial education. The curriculum of the elementary schools was broadened to include more of the real studies and their educational goals were, theoretically at least, no longer restricted to the narrow outlook characteristic of a colonial school pattern which had been dominated by ultra-conservative religious orders. The same was true of secondary education and, more particularly, of normal schools. Irma Wilson has analyzed the reforms of the nineteenth century in detail and shows that that period did make fundamental contributions in redirecting educational thought.[10] Yet, while it is true that the latter part of the century paved the way for the development of public education, and while much of present-day educational theory arose at that time, it required a bloody revolution and a subsequent period of thought and trial before these theoretical gains began to be felt on a large scale by the nation as a whole.

It is to be noted that secondary education in the nineteenth century was essentially of a collegiate and preparatory type and that it was definitely directed towards the professions established by tradition. Because of this, these schools cannot be regarded as contributing very much towards raising the general level of popular enlightenment. The exclusive tendency of such schools is made even more evident when it is realized that, in the main, secondary schools prepared not for a liberal higher education but for narrowly academic professional careers, though part of the secondary school program was professedly liberal in character. In the higher schools, even such fields of study as engineering and pharmacy were reduced to academic treatment, as the development of laboratory procedures was still the exception rather than the rule. In both secondary and higher education, the influence of the limited realism introduced into those levels of

10 Wilson, *op. cit.*

education by the Jesuits can still be seen and it is clear that science in education was more a matter of theory than of practice. Nevertheless, at least the beginnings were made in science and in broadly realistic studies. Some secondary schools offered courses in such fields as mechanical drawing, bookkeeping, zoology, and geography alongside such traditional courses as metaphysics and ethics. The higher schools, too, were beginning to respond to a changing social and economic order which was creating a demand for technical and professional specializations—in engineering, in the natural sciences, in business administration, etc.,—that is, demands other than those envisioned by the faculties of the traditional colleges.

One salient characteristic of the educational practices inherited from the nineteenth century can be seen in a failure to develop education as a professional career. This failure is not peculiar to Mexico but is evident in most of the countries of Latin America. From the very beginnings of public education in Mexico, school administration and the formulation of educational policy has been in the hands either of political figures who have had only a passing interest in education as a career or of those academic specialists whose limited experience as teachers was seldom supplemented by a broad study of educational theory and practice. The administrative and directive positions in education, instead of being filled by trained and experienced educators from the ranks of a teaching profession, have been assigned as rewards to those in the political world or, on occasion, to some learned person who had attained distinction as a literary figure—to a lawyer, a physician, or someone in a field of endeavor which, though of value in its own right, can seldom constitute a wholly adequate background for the successful discharge of the functions involved in educational administration. This practice has produced a distressing and puzzling lack of continuity in Mexican education. Each administrator or administration, because of this very lack of professional background in education, has relied on individual intuition and untrained interpretation in making far-reaching decisions as to the course which education should take. Each succeeding administration has felt it incumbent upon it to modify the program of its predecessor to conform to its peculiar, and usually equally untrained, viewpoint. As Ernest Gruening, describing recent events, has said in this connection: [11]

. . . The ephemeral character of much of Mexico's reconstructive effort renders the data of a given moment meaningless. A school opened one

[11] Gruening, op. cit., pp. 527–528.

year may be closed the next—even before the ink that described it had dried. A policy adopted by one executive may be—and often is—scrapped by his successor . . . A scientific and complete survey of Mexican education is, therefore, an impossibility for any one person because time and its changes would invalidate his efforts before he had completed his circuit.

The above weakness and defect, in Mexico, as in other parts of Latin America, is in part understandable, since education as a career has been limited largely to elementary education. The extensive interest in primary education manifested in the latter part of the nineteenth century and the relatively widespread establishment of normal schools at that time laid the basis for the recognition of the career of the elementary teacher by the public and its officials. That interest and effort and recognition is lacking, however, in secondary and higher education. In those fields the teacher is a subject-matter specialist, equipped only for whatever his specialty may be, and having little interest or understanding to bring to the educative process as a whole. The teachers in the schools above the elementary level are employed to teach a given class or subject. Their salary is computed on a class-hour basis and, in general, their responsibilities to the students or the school do not extend beyond the given class.

This specialization and compartmenting of teaching personnel makes it imperative for teachers in the upper levels of education to obtain employment in their respective specialties in a number of institutions if they are to command sufficient remuneration from teaching to make a living. Some professional and business men teach a class or two in a secondary school or college as an avocation or sideline to their private careers. That is to say that, as the phrase is understood in the United States, Mexico has not had and does not now have secondary or university faculties nor are the careers of secondary and university teachers recognized as professional. This has many important implications for the development of education in Mexico. These implications will be discussed in a later chapter. For the moment, it is to be noted that this failure to develop an educational profession on the secondary and higher levels of education has contributed greatly to the lack of a trained leadership for the administrative and policy-making positions in the educational programs of the several states and of the nation.

The explanation of the above-noted weaknesses involves numerous factors. European practice, borrowed without adaptation, has played an important part in developing this tradition. Financial limitations have also contributed. It is worthy of note, however, that such weaknesses are in large part due to the transfer of the function of education from Church to State. In the colonial pattern, when education was a function of the Church, a professional teaching personnel existed in the several religious orders that exercised the educational function. This meant that all phases of educational endeavor—organization and administration, methodology, supervision, etc.—received professional attention by those who had been especially prepared to educate. The transfer of education from Church to State in eliminating the religious control of education also eliminated the professional educator and the professional organization and leadership needed in a planned and efficient direction of educational programs. This forced the state to improvise not only educational personnel but also organization and direction. This process of improvisation is in large measure responsible for the disorganized and almost chaotic educational record that has extended from the earliest days of the Republic to the latter part of the nineteenth century. As has already been noted, the needs in the elementary fields began to be met late in the nineteenth century through the impulse given to the establishment of elementary schools and of centers for the preparation of teachers. However, the same is not true of secondary and higher education and the practice of improvising professional personnel at those levels has continued to the present time. The University, the National School for Teachers, and a higher normal school or two have in recent years been making small inroads into this situation but, insofar as the professionalization of upper-division teachers is concerned, it is still a far cry from the systematized efficiency of such professional educators as the Jesuits to the intuitive educational speculation of the part-time subject-matter specialists of the present day. This deficiency in Mexican education accounts for much of the lack of continuity of policies and procedures in the secondary and higher schools of Mexico. This is a major problem that Latin America inherited from the nineteenth century and from the transfer of education from Church to State.

VOCATIONAL AND TECHNICAL EDUCATION

Mention has been made in Chapter II of the magnificent efforts exerted on behalf of realistic and useful education in the sixteenth century. The activities of Bishop Vasco de Quiroga and of Fray Pedro de Gante as well as the educational programs of schools such as the Colegio de San

Juan de Letrán represented a clear recognition of the need for the vocational and technical preparation of students in the light of the realities of the Mexican scene. Unfortunately, these efforts and activities did not survive the sixteenth century and were not accepted as the basis for later development and expansion. It is true that individual missionaries here and there in New Spain made repeated attempts to follow in the footsteps of the great leaders of the sixteenth century. These attempts, though serving to perpetuate the memory of an education that was not based on verbalism and that sought to fit the student for real life, were not widespread enough to have established a recognized tradition—that is, a tradition which might have served as the foundation upon which to build a state or national edifice.

As a matter of fact, vocational and technical education has, until recently, been in disrepute and could not compete with the social prestige enjoyed by the humanities, law, and medicine. Even today, Mexican authorities often divide higher education into *"educación universitaria"* and *"educación técnica."* The former phrase usually connotes higher education in the liberal arts, law, medicine, and the natural sciences offered in a university organized group of colleges or faculties, while *educación técnica,* usually refers to technical education offered by colleges—or even by organized group of colleges with several faculties—not associated with an established university even though certain fields of study (engineering, the natural sciences, and the biological sciences, for example) may be the same in both types of institutions. This very confusion of the scope of "university education" is bringing about the realization that, in the modern world, higher education is not limited to the fields recognized in the traditional "faculties" but extends to the scientific and technical professions as well— that is, that the old meanings of "university" and "university education" have undergone a change in keeping with the progress of the times. The point, however, is that there is still an observable resistance to dignifying technical education by conferring on it the prestige which heretofore has been monopolized by the traditional universities and the fields of study which they embraced.

An attempt was made in 1843 to revive vocational education with the establishment of the Escuela de Artes y Oficios and a school of agriculture. Since the schools were not edquately financed, the former soon closed its doors and the latter continued operating with indifferent success. The Escuela de Artes y Oficios was reëstablished in 1856. It offered training in carpentry, cabinet-making, and ironwork. A special building was constructed for it and students were brought in from various parts of the country to be educated at government expense. When the students were given the privilege of enrolling in other institutions they deserted this vocational training to enroll at the University! The vocational school again closed its doors, to be revived once more in 1867 and rehabilitated in 1877 and still again in 1907—the program of studies, meanwhile, undergoing continual major revisions. This school, struggling under frequent reforms and uncertain support, continued to function until it was finally reorganized definitely as a higher technical and professional school in 1915. The then Secretary of Education, Félix Palavicini, who was an engineer, in reorganizing the school also created the Escuela Práctica for the preparation of mechanical and electrical engineers—a school that may be regarded as the first center of higher professional learning in technological fields in Mexico.

In 1871 an Escuela Nacional de Artes y Oficios was created to offer courses to girls in domestic activities and, in 1902, the commercial school for girls, Escuela "Miguel Lerdo de Tejada," was opened. Other similar centers as well as industrial schools for girls were established at later dates. All these schools, as well as the several vocational schools for boys, have undergone repeated changes from the time of their establishment to the present day. Their educational level has fluctuated over a range which, in the United States, comprises the intermediate grades of the elementary school and the junior college.

Soon after the reëstablishment of the Secretariat of Education in 1921, a department was created therein for the control of technical education. This department early began to seek to cordinate the heretofore unrelated vocational schools and to organize a well-planned system of technical education. Various progressive reforms were instituted between then and 1940, notably those of 1926, 1931, and 1936. In 1940, the plan of organization and control of these schools was again revised and some changes were made in curricula. At that time, all post-primary education below the vocational, specialization and college preparatory levels was recognized as secondary education and assigned to a department of *segunda enseñanza* in the Secretariat.[12] This was a highly significant move as it marks the first clear-cut demarcation of that level of education and, insofar as the plan for a national system of public schools is concerned, may be regarded

[12] See note, p. 89r

as the inauguration of modern, popular secondary education in Mexico. *Segunda enseñanza* is the first part of secondary education (grades 7, 8, 9), the other part (grades 10 and 11) being covered in the *vocacionales* or in the *preparatorias*.[13]

The 1940 reforms created an office (Dirección) of higher education and scientific research in the Secretariat. This office was divided into departments among which were those in charge of "higher technical education," "higher university education," teacher-education, scientific research, and the National Institute of Anthropology and History. The function of the department of higher technical education was that of the administering the Instituto Politécnico Nacional, a technological institute of higher learning that had evolved out of the Escuela Politécnica which was created for existing schools in 1931, and which had been reorganized again in 1937, when it was given its present name.

The Instituto Politécnico Nacional[14] is composed of several vocational (pre-professional) schools, offering both terminal vocational and college-preparatory (technical) courses, and six higher technical schools or faculties which lead to professional degrees. The pre-professional schools, enrolling 2,723 students in 1941, offered vocational courses for careers in construc-

---

[13] *"Segunda enseñanza,"* as recognized in Mexico, is post-primary but cannot be regarded as closely related to higher education so will not be elaborated upon herein. This level of education corresponds to that of junior high schools in the United States and embraces several types of schools—pre-vocational *secundarias* (22, with 10,545 students), which are three-year exploratory schools leading to the vocational schools; *secundarias* for workers (45, with 4,837 students) three-year schools with varied programs in vocational and general education for laborers and their children—some schools have night classes and some are boarding schools; *secundarias de cultura general* (145, with 21,055 students), and three-year schools for general academic education leading to the *preparatorias* for higher education. The curricula of these schools are flexible enough so that in any one of the above a student may get terminal elementary vocational training or prepare for entrance to a vocational or an academic preparatory school (the vocational schools are both terminal and preparatory technical schools, as noted above in the description of the Instituto Politécnico). In addition, *segunda enseñanza* embraces beginning agricultural education (both terminal and preparatory to higher agricultural schools) in 17 schools enrolling over 2,186 students. For further details see: Secretaría de Educación Pública, *Memoria, 1940–1941,* pp. 69–125.

The National University maintains an "Escuela Nacional de Iniciación Universitaria" which offers both day and night classes at this level—grades 7, 8, and 9. This school is, in effect, an academic junior high school. The Schools of Commerce and of Fine Arts of the University also offer beginning courses in their respective fields at this level of instruction.

[14] For generally descriptive data see: Secretaría de Educación Nacional, Departamento de Enseñanza Técnica, *Instituto Politécnico Nacional, Anuario,* Mexico, 1939, 87 pp.; and the mimeographed bulletin "Planes de Estudios De Las Carreras Que Se Cursan En El Instituto Politécnico Nacional 1940" issued by the same (now extinct) department. Caution should be exercised in the use of these sources as, due to later reforms of the school, they are no longer accurately descriptive of present enrollments, courses, or departments and schools.

tion work, mechanics, electricity, bookkeeping, filing (archivist), nursing, midwifery, and for various types of work in the textile industry. The professional schools of the Institute are those of mechanical and electrical engineering, with 814 students; textile engineering, enrolling 96 students; biological sciences, with 539 students; homeopathic medicine, 124 students; economic, political, and social sciences, with 824 students; and architectural engineering, with 268 students. It is of interest to note that the school of biological sciences has inaugurated the career of rural "medic" which requires a period of field practice as part of the obligatory interneship. This school also has a well-organized department of anthropology which works in close harmony not only with the University and the Instituto Nacional de Antropología e Historia, but with institutions in the United States and in the countries of Central America (through fellowships, exchange professors, etc.).

While the general critique of higher education and research in Mexico will be reserved for the next chapter, it is well to note at this point that, with due allowances for certain weaknesses inherent in the administrative organization and control of this institution, the Instituto Politécnico is the outstanding Mexican educational institution of higher learning and research in the applied arts and sciences.[15] The institute is coeducational. Field and laboratory research activities form an important part of the work of both students and faculty. Particular attention is given to those researches—in entomology, botany, anthropology, etc.—which give promise of meeting vital needs in Mexican life—as regards agriculture, Indian population, public health and sanitation, etc. This school bids well to fill a crucial gap in the intellectual leadership of the nation—the gap which has resulted from the traditional disdain with which higher education has viewed Mexican realities, and from the intellectual monopoly exercised by the traditional faculties.

The importance of the Instituto Politécnico and of other higher technical schools is made evident by the fact that, of the 11,213 professional degrees granted by all Mexican institutions up to 1930, almost 9,000 were in law

---

15 The interpretations and descriptions offered in this study, except where specified, do not account for the changes which have taken place since November, 1941. Recent changes in the Secretariat and in governmental policy have resulted in certain important reforms, *i.e.,* the disavowal of coeducation and the reduction of the scope and function of the Instituto Politécnico. The significance of these reforms and the degree to which they will be effected is yet a matter of conjecture.

and medicine and only 1,910 were in engineering.[16] In spite of this, the census of 1930 made it evident that over 6,000 persons were practicing engineering—that is, over 4,000 without suitable training, even when it is assumed that all who had degrees were practicing their profession—and ignoring the fact that a small number of practitioners may have obtained degrees in foreign countries. In like manner, there was a difference of about 6,000 between the number of degrees granted in medicine and the number of practitioners. Only 335 degrees were recorded in pharmacy, but there were almost 3,000 practicing pharmacists. There were 124 degrees in electrical and mechanical engineering and 925 exercising those careers. Out of a total of 6,444 degrees granted by the National University between 1929 and 1940, the first ten professions in numerical importance were:

Medicine (surgery)	2,481
Law	1,346
Dentistry	607
Midwifery	507
Civil Engineering	351
Chemistry (Pharmacy)	237
Accountancy	115
Veterinary medicine	96
Chemistry	74
Chemical engineering	70

During the period 1901–1939 (see lists in following section), the higher institutions of Mexico granted 56,595 degrees, half of which (28,853) were for the teaching profession. The degrees in law numbered 5,380 and those in medicine 5,869. There were less than 2,500 degrees granted in engineering (of these, 821 went to civil engineers). Nursing was the career next in rank on the basis of the number of degrees, with 1,131, and pharmacy followed, with 778. In examining Professor Mendizábal's detailed statistical compilations (unpublished), it is worthy of note that, of the 3,023 professional degrees granted in 1939, 1,657 were from institutions in the Federal District, and that institutions for every state are represented among the rest—Durango, Chihuahua, and Chiapas leading with 142, 130, and 111 degrees respectively.

The growth of vocational secondary schools in the last few years should

[16] These and following related data were obtained through the courtesy of Professor Miguel O. de Mendizábal.

bring about a decided increase in the number of students pursuing higher degrees in technical fields. In 1935, there were 380 technical, commercial, industrial, and arts and trades schools in the nation with an enrollment of over 35,000 students. Later statistics are not available for the nation as a whole but, in the light of the increased activity manifested in this field, it can be assumed that the enrollment figures have shown a decided in-crease during the last five years. The creation of new-type schools, for special purposes, is adding to the numbers in non-academic secondary schools. The School For Social Workers (in the Federal District), for example, enrolls over 600 girls in lower and upper secondary levels, while the preparatory residential school for workers' children, enrolling 600 students, serves in part as a preparatory school for the Instituto Politécnico.[17] Adult-education centers and night schols, also, are adding to the number of peo-ple receiving secondary and higher technical education.

This brief review of some of the salient aspects of technical and voca-tional education indicates the growing importance of that field of endeavor in Mexico. The figures cited suggest, nevertheless, that what has been done so far in this field is far from adequate in meeting the needs of the nation for trained personnel in industry, commerce, the trades, and other technical and specialized vocations. Though accurate figures on this point are not available, it can safely be estimated that the total enrollment in technical, agricultural, and trades and industrial courses in all vocational (upper secondary) and higher institutions in the nation is less than 100,000. It is doubtful if such enrollment totals more than half that number. When the critical problems facing the nation—in industrial development, the incorporation of indigenous peoples, agriculture, etc.—are taken into ac-count, the true magnitude of Mexican shortcomings in technical educa-tion becomes apparent. At the same time, the progress made in the last few years in the creation, organization, support, and encouragement of this phase of education assumes larger significance than school statistics alone would indicate.

COLLEGE PREPARATORY AND "UNIVERSITY" EDUCATION

It has already been stated that, though the nineteenth century witnessed many attempts to extend educational opportunity to large numbers of the common people and to make higher education responsive to the realities confronting the nation, these efforts did not reach fruition and, at best,

[17] Secretaría de Educación Pública. *Memoria, 1940–1941*, p. 139.

served merely to augment interest in educational reforms. The colleges inherited from the colony—among them San Juan de Letrán, San Ildefonso, San Gregorio, and Santa María de Todos Santos—underwent numerous reforms from the very beginnings of independence.[18] Most of them faded out of existence before the end of the century. In various parts of the nation several of the colonial schools were perpetuated in the form of the new schools which were founded upon their ruins—as was the case when San Ildefonso became the locus for the establishment of the National Preparatory School. A few others, notably San Nicolás at Morelia, survived the century and have maintained their identity to the present time. In the main, however, the nineteenth century did not seize upon the colonial institutions as a nucleus around which to build national schools. Rather, it chose to scrap the old institutions and to experiment with its own creations.

The early educational attempts of independent Mexico were largely projects "on paper." The unsettled state of affairs during the first forty-five years of independence and the poverty of the nation relegated educational interests to the realm of theory rather than of practice. The restoration of the Republic in 1867, after the expulsion of the French, marks the beginnings of serious governmental efforts to establish public education in Mexico. It was in 1867 that Gabino Barreda was charged with the task of creating the National Preparatory School. The founding of that school represents a momentous milestone in the development of Mexican secondary and higher education. That event was the occasion for the expression of a new educational philosophy in Mexico, a philosophy which broke completely with the fusion of narrow humanism and limited realism inherited from the colony. The creation of this new school also served as a strong stimulus to the several state governments and they, too, were soon engaged in the establishment of preparatory and higher schools.

By the latter part of the nineteenth century, the state and federal governments supported some fifty-five institutions of higher learning, distributed over twenty-eight states.[19] All of these schools offered college preparatory courses and most of them offered fields of higher professional study, principally law, engineering, and medicine. In addition, there were some twenty-five seminaries for the training of clergymen which offered the

[18] Blair, op. cit., pp. 268–291.
[19] See: Jose Díaz Covarrubias, La Instrucción Pública en México. México, Imprenta de Gobierno, 1875, pp. 3–217.

usual program of studies embracing such subjects as theology, canon law, Latin, philosophy, metaphysics, and mathematics. There were other private secondary schools and colleges as well as several public institutions of a special nature. However, in all of these institutions, public and private, the total enrollment (including preparatory school students) of men in 1874 was less than fifteen thousand and that of women was less than three thousand. Irma Wilson, summarizing the statistics for 1884, cites the following: [20]

The record of achievement of the twenty-seven states, the territory of Lower California, and the Federal District as pictured by Antonio García Cubas in his *Cuadro geográfico, estadístico, descriptivo e histórico de los Estados Unidos Mexicanos,* published in 1884, shows considerable growth in point of numbers of the free schools for the decade following that covered by the report of Covarrubias. There is a total of 8,536 schools: 6,441 for boys and 2,095 for girls. Thirty-seven per cent of the entire number are located in the states of Puebla, Mexico, Vera Cruz, and in the Federal District. In addition the Sociedad Catolica supports 44 free schools, which 3,695 students attend, raising the total number of free schools to 8,580, with an attendance of 439,648. This does not include the *amigas* which are not free.

The distribution of establishments at the secondary and professional level is as follows: 16 Preparatory schools; 15 Secondary schools for girls; 3 of Arts and Trades; 19 of Jurisprudence; 9 of Medicine; 8 of Engineering; 4 of Fine Arts; 1 of Agriculture; 1 of Commerce; 3 Conservatories of Music; 26 Seminaries; and 31 Liceos and Institutes; or a total of 136 institutions. In addition to these there are a Practice School of Mines in Pachuca, Schools for the Deaf and Dumb and for the Blind in the capital, the Colegio Militar in Chapultepec, the Nautical Schools at Campeche and Mazatlán, and the Practice School of Agriculture in Acapantzingo. Attending these 143 establishments are 16,809 students: 14,438 men and 2,371 women. This represents only a fraction of the entire number because there are no data for the private institutions.

The broad vision which inspired the founding of the National Preparatory School in 1867 promised a redirection of secondary education into new, realistic, and popular paths. That promise was premature, however, and that great institution, the successor to the old Colegio de San Ildefonso

[20] Wilson, *op. cit.,* pp. 254–255.

of the Jesuits, soon reverted to the traditional verbalism. Alfonso Reyes, in reviewing the "immediate past," recalls his studies there and analyzes their drawbacks in the education of his generation—the "generation of the Centenary," the intellectuals of the Revolution.[21] Reyes points out that the school's original and encyclopaedic program of studies had been based by the founder, Barreda, who had been a pupil of Comte, on Comte's positivistic conception of personal development and social reform. That program comprised a broad scientific and humanistic general education and sought to prepare the student for reasoned humanitarian social action. The school soon degenerated from its highly liberal purpose, giving way to the "mechanisms of method." Mathematics, natural history, science, and even the humanities themselves became dry, academic disciplines. As Alfonso Reyes points out (p. 16), "There is nothing so poor as the natural history, the human history or the literature that were studied in that School in the days of the Centenary" (1910). Laboratory equipment was almost abandoned, and science was largely a mental discipline. So with the rest of the curriculum, and the school, the people's college, became but a mental exercise ground that served only as a stepping stone to the professional schools.

Gabino Barreda envisioned a broadly liberal and scientific program of secondary education which was to perform a much larger function than that of preparing students for the professional schools. However, as indicated above, it was not long before the National Preparatory School became strictly a college-preparatory. The original broad significance of "preparatory" was soon lost sight of, and preparatory schools were thought of exclusively as the initial grade in higher education. This limited interpretation has persisted to the present day and pupils in the *preparatorias* study specialized curricula all of which leads to the bachelor's degree (*bachillerato*) and to a given faculty in the professional schools.

Before the organization of the *secundarias* (see preceding section), the preparatory schools were organized around five-year, post-primary curricula. Since, at that time, the entire secondary school level was found within these strictly college-preparatory institutions which were, by their very nature, few in number, this meant that popular secondary education was virtually non-existent in Mexico. The creation of *secundarias* for general-education purposes as well as the expansion of prevocational schools (both are three-year, post-primary schools) caused the *preparatorias* to

[21] Reyes, *op. cit.*, pp. 11–25.

limit their programs to the last two years of the secondary level. The programs of the *vocacionales* (vocational schools) parallel those of the *preparatorias* and, as already stated, prepare their students for trades and for the higher technical schools.

The merits of this arrangement are obvious. From several standpoints, this system of secondary education is superior to the plans prevalent in the United States, where secondary schools (junior and senior high schools) attempt to perform all three functions—vocational and technical education, general education, and academic education—usually with the result that the academic (college-preparatory) aim takes precedence over the others.

The Secretariat of Education operates four preparatory schools. One of these, at Coyoacán in the Federal District, is a residential school for workers' children. It has an enrollment of 600 students. Three preparatory schools are maintained on the nation's northern border, one at Piedras Negras, Coahuila; one at Nuevo Laredo, Tamaulipas; and one at Nogales, Sonora. Each of the seven universities of the nation maintains at least one preparatory school. These universities, and their subdivisions are: [22]

I. UNIVERSIDAD NACIONAL AUTONOMA DE MEXICO, Mexico, D. F.[23]

    a. National Preparatory School (former Colegio de San Ildefonso).

    b. Faculty of Philosophy and Letters.

    c. Faculty of Sciences.

    d. Faculty of Law and Social Sciences;

        (1) National School of Jurisprudence,

        (2) National School of Economics,

        (3) National School of Commerce and Administration.

    e. Faculty of Medicine;

        (1) National School of Medicine (with sections on Nursing and Obstetrics),

        (2) National School of Odontology,

        (3) National School of Veterinary Medicine.

    f. Faculty of Engineering and Chemical Sciences;

        (1) School of Engineering,

        (2) National School of Chemical Sciences.

[22] Most of the data for this listing of institutions and for the list that follows, which the writer was unable to locate at any other source, were obtained from the files of the National University through the courtesy of Dr. José Torres Torija, Secretary of that institution.

[23] The history and organization of this institution has been included in detail in the preceding chapter.

g. Faculty of Fine Arts;
   (1) National School of Architecture,
   (2) National School of Plastic Arts.
h. National School of University Initiation (or Extension).[24]

2. UNIVERSIDAD DE MICHOACAN, Morelia, Michoacán.

   a. Preparatory School (Colegio de San Nicolás Hidalgo).
   b. Faculty of Medicine.
   c. Faculty of Jurisprudence.
   d. Faculty of Engineering.
   e. Faculty of Fine Arts.

3. UNIVERSIDAD DE YUCATAN, Mérida, Yucatán.

   a. Literary Institution of the State (preparatory).
   b. Faculty of Medicine and Surgery and Schools of Nursing and Midwifery.
   c. Faculty of Jurisprudence.
   d. Faculty of Chemistry and Pharmacy.

4. UNIVERSIDAD OFICIAL DE GUADALAJARA, Guadalajara, Jalisco.

   a. Preparatory School for Boys.
   b. Preparatory School for Girls.
   c. Commercial School for Girls.
   d. National School for Teachers.
   e. National School of Jurisprudence.
   f. National School of Medicine.
   g. National School of Pharmacy.

5. UNIVERSIDAD AUTONOMA DE GUADALAJARA, Guadalajara, Jalisco.

   a. Preparatory School.
   b. Faculty of Law and Social Sciences.
   c. Faculty of Medicine.
   d. Faculty of Odontology.
   e. Faculty of Engineering.
   f. Faculty of Commerce.
   g. Faculty of Chemical Sciences.

[24] See footnote, page 89.

6. UNIVERSIDAD DE PUEBLA, Puebla, Puebla.

    a. Preparatory School.
    b. School of Medicine.
    c. School of Commerce.
    d. School of Nursing.
    e. School of Obstetrics.
    f. School of Engineering.
    g. School of Law and Social Sciences.
    h. School of Chemistry and Pharmacy.

7. UNIVERSIDAD SOCIALISTA DE CULIACAN, Culiacán, Sinaloa.

    a. Preparatory School (at Mazatlán).
    b. Normal School.
    c. School of Commerce.
    d. School of Engineering.
    e. School of Pharmacy.
    f. School of Laws.

8. UNIVERSIDAD OBRERA DE MEXICO, Coyoacán, D. F.

(This is not organized into schools or faculties but is a part-time continuation institution offering special courses to workers. The Preparatory School for Workers' Children, mentioned above, may be regarded as the preparatory school for this institution. However, the Preparatory School is under the Secretariat of Education whereas the Workers University is under the general supervision of the Labor Department of the Government.)

The other public, upper-secondary and higher schools in Mexico (with the exception of those mentioned in the preceding section and those teacher-training and special schools dealt with in the succeeding section) are, by political subdivisions:

1. AGUASCALIENTES: a. State Preparatory and Commercial School, Aguascalientes.

2. BAJA CALIFORNIA: a. The Normal and Preparatory School, Mexicali.

3. CAMPECHE: a. "Instituto Campechano," Campeche.
                     b. State Normal School, Campeche.

c. Official School of Jurisprudence, Campeche.

d. "Liceo Carmelita," Ciudad del Carmen.

4. CHIAPAS:
a. State Normal and Preparatory School, Tuxtla Gutierrez.

b. Regional Preparatory School, San Cristóbal las Casas.

c. School of Jurisprudence, San Cristóbal las Casas.

d. Preparatory School of Soconusco, Tapachula.

5. CHIHUAHUA:
a. State Preparatory School, Chihuahua.

b. State Normal School, Chihuahua.

c. School of Agriculture, Ciudad Juárez.

6. COAHUILA:
a. Preparatory School of the East, Saltillo.

b. State Normal School, Saltillo.

c. "Ateneo Fuente," with a preparatory school, Saltillo.

d. Preparatory School, Campo Redondo.

e. Preparatary School, La Laguna.

7. COLIMA:
a. Preparatory and Normal School, Colima.

8. DURANGO:
a. "Instituto Juárez," with preparatory and professional instruction, Durango.

b. Normal School, with preparatory and professional instruction, Durango.

9. GUANAJUATO:
a. Preparatory School, Guanajuato.

b. Primary Normal School, Guanajuato.

c. School of Engineering, Guanajuato.

d. School of Laws, Guanajuato.

e. School of Pharmacy, Guanajuato.

f. School of Nursing and Obstetrics, Guanajuato.

g. Preparatory and Secondary School, León.

h. Preparatory School, Guanajuato.

i. "Instituto Colón," Guanajuato.

10. GUERRERO:
a. Secondary and Normal School, Chilpancingo.

11. HIDALGO:
a. Literary and Scientific Institute, Pachuca.

12. MEXICO:
a. Literary and Scientific Institute, Toluca;
    (1) School of Commerce,
    (2) Normal School for Teachers,
    (3) Normal School for Girls.

13. MORELOS:
a. Preparatory School "Bachilleratos," Cuernavaca.

14. NAYARIT:
a. State Institute, Tepic;
    (1) Preparatory School,
    (2) Normal School,
    (3) Commercial School,
    (4) School of Fine Arts,
    (5) School of Arts and Trades.

15. NUEVO LEON:
a. Preparatory School, Monterrey.
b. "Instituto Laurens," Monterrey.
c. School of Medicine, Monterrey.
d. School of Nursing, Monterrey.
e. School of Jurisprudence, Monterrey.
f. School of Painting, Monterrey.

16. OAXACA:
a. Autonomous Institute of Arts and Sciences, with day and night preparatory schools and academies leading to professions, Oaxaca.
b. State Normal School, Oaxaca.
c. Regional Normal School of the Isthmus, Juchitan.

17. PUEBLA:
a. State Normal Institute with primary, preparatory, and professional courses, Puebla.

18. QUERETARO:
a. State Civil College, with preparatory, commercial courses, and School of Laws, Queretaro.
b. "Centro Educativo de Queretaro," Queretaro.
c. Civil College (Chemistry and Pharmacy), Queretaro.

19. SAN LUIS POTOSI:
a. College of San Luís Potosí (preparatory), San Luís Potosí.
b. Preparatory School, Río Verde.
c. Preparatory English College, San Luís Potosí.

20. SONORA: a. State Normal School, Hermosillo.

21. TABASCO: a. Normal School.
b. "Instituto Juárez," (preparatory), Villahermosa.

22. TAMAULIPAS: a. Normal and Preparatory School, Ciudad Victoria.
b. Secondary, Normal, and Preparatory School, Tampico.
c. Secondary and Preparatory School, Matamoros.
d. Preparatory School, Tampico.

23. VERACRUZ: a. Secondary and Preparatory School, Jalapa.
b. Secondary and Preparatory School, Veracruz.
c. Secondary and Arts and Trades School, Córdoba.
d. School of Arts and Trades, Jalapa.
e. State School of Law, Jalapa.
f. School of Nursing and Obstetrics, Jalapa.
g. "Universidad Libre Veracruzana," Nogales.

24. ZACATECAS: a. Institute of Sciences, Zacatecas.
b. Normal School, Zacatecas.
c. Rural Normal School, Río Grande.

The Federal Government, through the Secretariat of Education, has been granting financial assistance to some of these institutions though it exercises no direct control over their programs or policies. In 1940–41, the following grants were made: [25]

1. Universidad Nacional	$3,000,000.00 (pesos)
2. Universidad Obrera	300,000.00
3. Universidad de Michoacán	50,000.00
4. Universidad de Guadalajara	100,000.00
5. Universidad de Yucatán	25,000.00
6. Universidad de Veracruz	25,000.00
7. Colegio de México [26]	300,000.00
8. Escuela Normal de Jalisco	25,000.00
9. Escuela Normal de Zacatecas	8,000.00
10. Instituto de Ciencias y Artes de Oaxaca	50,000.00
11. Instituto de San Luis Potosi	75,000.00
12. Instituto de Zacatecas	8,000.00
Total	$3,966,000.00

[25] Secretaría de Educación Pública. *Memoria, 1940–1941,* p. 140.
[26] To be treated later in this chapter.

The National University, though autonomous since 1929, has continued to receive yearly grants from the government and will, in all probability, continue to receive them in the future. The other grants listed above are of more recent origin and, though they will probably be repeated yearly, there is less certainty about this than in the case of the National University. All the grants appear to be free of any direct attempt by the government to control the institutions or to guide their policies.

There is no record available of the number of *bachilleratos* (bachelor degrees) given by the preparatory schools. The same is true for the other types of upper-secondary schools. This absence of data is due to the fact that there is no central clearing house for educational statistics in Mexico, for data on the schools of the several states and territories is not incorporated in the reports of the Secretariat of Education. These reports are limited to descriptions of federal schools. In addition to the state and federal schools, there are a number of private secondary schools in Mexico. Most of these are either commercial or academic schools. Though these schools are subject to federal inspection and while some of them have associated themselves with one of the universities, there is no report which describes them.

From an examination of various sources it appears that in 1927 there were 79 secondary and preparatory schools in the nation with an enrollment of about 17,000 students. By 1935 the number of schools had increased to 164 and the enrollment was around 26,000. This last enrollment figure has undoubtedly been considerably increased in the last six years and it can be estimated that the present enrollment at this level of education is in the neighborhood of 50,000. It should be noted that this estimate includes the enrollment in *secundarias,* but not that in the technical upper-secondary schools nor in the agricultural and teacher-training schools of this level. This indicates that the present enrollment in the preparatory-type schools is less than 15,000 and that the number of *bachilleratos* granted in any one year is less than 7,000.

The activity of the institutions of higher learning is suggested by the following list of degrees granted:

PROFESSIONAL TITLES AND DEGREES
GRANTED IN MEXICO [27]

Professions	1930	1939	1901 to 1939
Lawyer	138	289	5,380
Agronomist			159
Architect	6	18	205
Doctor of Philosophy and Letters			8
Dental Surgeon	44	72	1,053
Primary Teacher	12	85	778
Nurse	62	71	1,131
Pharmacist	13	38	571
Agronomical Engineer	46	4	239
Civil Engineer	17	52	821
Mechanical and Electrical Engineer	15	56	336
Mines and Metallurgical Engineer	4	12	182
Petroleum Engineer		3	13
Chemical Engineer	3	7	117
Topographical and Hydrographical Engineer	3	5	342
Engineer (others)	14	3	364
Licentiate in Economy		6	14
Rural Teacher	157	184	1,630
Medical Surgeon and Obstetrician	205	333	6,069
Midwife	103	71	1,912
Professor "Especialista"		121	2,111
Professor of Elementary Primary Instruction	462	8	3,704
Professor of Superior Primary Instruction	122	848	16,086
University Professor		7	525
Chemist	15	84	410
Veterinary	15	6	205
Others	310	640	12,230
Totals	1,766	3,023	56,595

Every state in the nation is represented in the above. The following list shows the number of degrees given in each state in 1939. Compare with the second column of figures in the preceding list.

[27] Data by courtesy of Miguel O. de Mendizábal.

TITLES AND DEGREES GIVEN IN 1939, BY STATES [28]

Aguascaliente	28
Campeche	22
Coahuila	58
Colima	14
Chiapas	111
Chihuahua	130
Dto. Federal	1,657
Durango	142
Guanajuato	46
Guerrero	2
Hidalgo	21
Jalisco	93
México	68
Michoacán	57
Morelos	7
Nayarit	7
Nuevo Leon	65
Oaxaca	26
Puebla	66
Querétaro	65
S. Luis Potosí	53
Sinaloa	12
Sonora	5
Tabasco	30
Tamaulipas	87
Tlaxcala	7
Veracruz	75
Yucatan	66
Zacatecas	3
Total	3,023

The degrees given by the University of Mexico in 1940 were the following: [29]

Title or Degree	Male	Female	Total
Medical Surgeon	256	13	269
Dental Surgeon	37	12	49
Medical Veterinary	8		8
Midwife		22	22

[28] Data by courtesy of Miguel O. de Mendizábal.

[29] From the newspaper *Novedades*, November 18, 1941. The grand total given in the press report was 686, instead of that indicated above.

Title or Degree	Male	Female	Total
Nurse		20	20
Licentiate in Law	150		150
Licentiate in Economics	2	1	3
Public Accountant and Auditor	12		12
Civil Engineer	43		43
Petroleum Engineer	2		2
Topographical and Hydrographical Engineer	5		5
Mechanical and Electrical Engineer	4		4
Forestry Engineer	1		1
Engineer of Mines and Metallurgy	2		2
Chemist	14	4	18
Chemical Engineer	9		9
Pharmaceutical and Biological Chemist	9	15	24
Metallurgical Assayer	2		2
Master in Mathematical Sciences	1		1
Doctor in Mathematical Sciences	1		1
Doctor in Geographical Sciences	1		1
Master in Geographical Sciences	1		1
Master in Sciences of Education	1	1	2
Doctor in Letters	1	1	2
Master in Biological Sciences	1		1
Architect	22		22
Master of Arts in Spanish	2	8	10
Master in Modern Languages		1	1
Totals	587	98	685

It has already been pointed out that teachers in the upper-secondary and higher schools are not on a full-time employment basis. The limitations of this practice are aggravated by the low-salary scales involved. This is illustrated by the fact that, for a class that meets for one hour three times a week, the usual monthly pay at the National University is eighty-one pesos. When it is realized that it would call for a salary of from 600 to 800 pesos a month for a professor to maintain a satisfactory standard of living in Mexico City, it becomes clear that this salary scale is not conducive to the best results in higher education. To receive 800 pesos for teaching, a professor would have to carry more than a 27-hour weekly load—that is, he would have to meet classes for four and one-half hours daily for six days a week! This is more than twice the normal load for a university instructor in the United States.

Under the above conditions, a university teacher in Mexico has little time for student conferences, examinations and reports, research, professional development (personal and institutional), etc. This is particularly true since every professor's preparation is narrowly specialized, and it would be rare for one institution to offer several sections of one course. Therefore, to teach nine classes, the teacher must be employed in several institutions which are widely distributed over the city—adding to the time load and deducting from professional service and study, to say nothing of the travel costs involved. The implications of this situation are obvious, for the above arrangement is not only impossible from the professional point of view but it is virtually impossible from the physical. To avoid it, the university teacher must content himself with fewer classes and a low standard of living or else find means, other than teaching, to supplement his income. In any case, higher education suffers.

An illustration of one of the effects of this situation is found in the examination of the teaching personnel of the several schools of the National University.[30] The Faculty of Jurisprudence is made up of about 120 members. The Preparatory School has over 175 teachers; the School of Chemical Sciences has 78; the Faculty of Sciences, about 50; the Faculty of Philosophy and Letters, 80; etc. This plethora of personnel results, among other things, in that the average number of classes taught by each individual in a given school is around two—for a monthly income, from that one school, of some 54 pesos. The range in the number of courses taught by one person in one school or faculty is from 1 to 5, and the salary from 27 to 135 pesos, roughly. Many professors teach in several schools or faculties of the University, but, as the employment of teaching personnel is not co-ordinated through central planning and administration, the positions held by these professors have the same status as though the employment were in several distinct institutions. All of this results in competition for *cátedras* (courses), the dilution of the teaching function among many professors, and consequent antagonism to full-time employment, etc. This vicious circle is an important phase of what this writer regards as the most serious defect in higher education in Mexico (and in Latin America)—a defect characterized, both in causes and effects, by administrative inefficiency; by a teaching personnel enslaved by inadequate remuneration and dispersed assignments which tend to reduce the teachers' effectiveness in rendering professional services; and by a point of view which regards educational services as purchasable on a piece-work basis. These conditions are so signifi-

[30] See: Universidad Nacional Autónoma De México. *Anuario* of which one is issued for each school or faculty.

cant for higher education that, though such a statement is not entirely true, it might be said that an educational profession for the teaching of higher learning is virtually non-existent in Mexico. Certainly, these conditions constitute a tremendous handicap to the development of higher education.

THE EDUCATION OF TEACHERS

The Colegio de San Juan de Letrán, founded in 1547, may be regarded as the first normal school in the New World. One of its principal functions at the time of its creation was that of preparing teachers. It should be noted, also, that Fray Pedro de Gante inaugurated a monitorial system by which he trained assistants to teach at his school of San José and elsewhere, both in Mexico City and in nearby towns. In spite of these auspicious beginnings, teacher education did not assume much importance until the last two decades of the nineteenth century. The normal schools that had existed prior to that time were small institutions which served more as general academic secondary schools than as centers for teacher education.[31]

The expansion of primary schools in the last decades of the nineteenth century produced a new interest in the development of normal schools. The work of the Swiss educator, Rébsamen, and of Justo Sierra is worthy of note in this connection.[32] Several new normal schools were created, both in the Federal District and in other parts of the Republic. The old normal schools revised their programs, giving more place to pedagogical subjects and activities. Modern methods were introduced and the use of "practice schools" became common. All in all, this period infused new life into teacher education and established the basis for the development of a teaching profession for primary schools.[33] These were small beginnings, however, for there were almost no schools in rural areas and the town schools were relatively few in number. It has already been stated that, as late as 1906, there were less than 800,000 children in all public and private schools in Mexico. This fact would indicate that the normal schools, limited largely to the training of teachers for primary schools, were highly restricted in their scope of action and, therefore, could not continue to develop as centers of learning until elementary education was given further encouragement. This did not take place until the Revolution, and it has been

[31] Sánchez, *op. cit.* (*Mexico—A Revolution by Education*), pp. 136-138.
[32] Edwin Zollinger, *Enrique C. Rébsamen.* Translated from the German by Solomon Kahan. Mexico, Secretaría de Educación Pública, 1935.
[33] See: Wilson, *op. cit.,* pp. 294-317.

only since 1921 that teacher education has begun to attain significance in Mexican higher education.

The rapid growth of primary schools since 1921, particularly in rural areas, created a demand for teachers which the existing normal schools could not meet. This demand forced upon the government the necessity of resorting to the employment of untrained personnel and, as a consequence, to the development of an empirical pedagogy in Mexico. This empiricism has been of inestimable value in giving a realistic trend to teacher education. As normal schools to meet the increased demands for teachers were created or as the old ones were reformed and expanded, the preparation of teachers, responding to the pressing needs which teachers were encountering in the field, has been shorn of much of its traditional verbalism and has been adjusted to the task of meeting the demands of a rapidly expanding system of mass education. This rapid growth, and its implications for teacher education, is best appreciated when the figures cited above for 1906 are compared with the following: [34]

The Government of the Republic and the Governments of the States are deeply preoccupied in diffusing and expanding the primary education at the people's service, both in the country and in the city. In effect, to date it has been possible to establish 13,358 primary schools which are maintained by the Federation; 7,420 by the States and Municipalities; 977 of mixed (State-Federal) support; 991 by agricultural, mining, and industrial organization in conformity with Article 123 of the Constitution; and 445 by private initiative. There function in the country a total of 23,191 schools, with an enrollment of 2,037,870 pupils, who are instructed by 46,653 teachers.

It should be stated that the greater part of the primary schools have established night classes for adults and that, in addition, there exist 91 federal schools which are especially dedicated to this service and which have 488 teachers and 8,760 pupils.

The sum which the Federal Government has assigned in the budget for the support of primary education during the present year amounts to $37,491,332.89.

The energetic efforts by the national Government to federalize education have tended to give teacher education for primary schools a semblance of unity. Today the public schools of the states of Oaxaca, Guerrero,

[34] Secretaría de Educación Pública, *op. cit.*, p. 13.

Morelos, Campeche, Tabasco, Nayarit, Colima, Querétaro, Chihuahua, Hidalgo, and México have been integrated into the program of the national system of schools. Elsewhere, the Secretariat of Education is seeking to serve as the coordinating and advisory agency, especially in the field of primary education. This assumption of responsibility for mass education by the national Government has placed a major responsibility for the preparation of teachers in the hands of the Secretariat of Education. Considerable effort is being expended in this direction through the creation of federal normal schools, the federalization of state-supported normal schools, the incorporation of private normal schools, and through the organization of teacher institutes and conferences which offer professional training and guidance to teachers in service.[35]

The Secretariat of Education operates 26 rural normal schools which are located in 20 political subdivisions of the nation. These schools enroll 3,263 students, of which 862 are girls. The students of these schools enter upon their program of studies in teacher education upon completing the six years of primary education. In addition, there are four schools which enroll primary-school students in grades 5 and 6 and which aim to prepare such students for entrance into the rural normal institutions of secondary-school level.

The National School for Teachers, in Mexico City, enrolls 1,234 students. At the same school, there is maintained the National Institute for Secondary School Teachers with an enrollment of some six hundred students.[36] The same institute maintains other teacher-education centers of the Republic, enrolling 284 pupils. A vigorous effort is being made, through short courses and institutes as well as through regular classes carried on at the National School for Teachers and other similar institutions, to bring about the preparation of secondary school teachers and, to some extent, the preparation of teachers for institutions of higher learning. There is a likelihood that these activities will in time be concentrated into a superior (postgraduate) normal school. With the exception already noted in the case of rural normal schools (four of which are of an upper primary level and the rest of secondary level) normal schools in Mexico are of post-secondary school level. It is intended, as has been suggested above, that in the near future a well organized postgraduate level of teacher education will develop. While statistics are not available on this point, there are already a few teachers receiving training at this postgraduate level.

[35] Secretaría de Educación Pública, *op. cit.*, pp. 141–166.   [36] Now a separate institution.

The increased activity in the preparation of teachers is illustrated by the figures cited by Watson.[37] In 1928 only 4,463 teachers of a total of 7,816 had any sort of normal-school or college title or degree. In 1936, of 17,895 teachers, 12,109 had titles or degrees. While these degrees were probably largely from institutions of secondary-school level, the increase is significant. Reference to the list of degrees granted in 1939, as included in the preceding section, makes it evident that 85 individuals received degrees as primary teachers, 184 as rural teachers, 121 as teachers of special subjects, 856 as elementary school teachers, and 7 as university teachers. All these were higher-education degrees. It should also be noted that the degrees granted by the Faculty of Sciences of the National University are, to a large extent, awarded to those who will teach in secondary or higher schools.

Teaching, as a profession, is slowly expanding from the elementary-school level to that of the secondary schools and, in a small way, to institutions of higher learning. The great progress made in the development of teacher education for elementary schools is slowly having salutary effects in the upper levels. The work that is now being done in introducing professional subjects into the program of studies for subject-matter specialists can be expected to become rapidly more widespread. The Faculty of Sciences of the National University requires that candidates for the degrees of Master, or Doctor of sciences shall have taken the courses in Educational Philosophy and Educational Psychology offered by the Faculty of Philosophy and Letters. Other faculties and schools are slowly recognizing that many of their graduates will become teachers and are beginning to allow for pedagogical courses and activities in their curricula. The fine start already made in the higher education of teachers by the National School for Teachers, the National Institute for Secondary School Teachers, and in numerous urban normal schools is slowly but surely creating the nucleus for a well-trained teaching profession. The expansion of secondary and higher schools, coupled with an increasing interest in teacher education on the part of the universities, is beginning to give encouragement and prestige to this important area of vital and basic instruction.

SPECIAL INSTITUTIONS

The last twenty years have seen Mexican higher education make many important breaks with classical humanism. Nearly every succeeding year

[37] Watson, *op. cit.,* p. 32.

has witnessed the establishing of a new type of center of higher learning or the reorganization, along realistic lines, of some verbalistic institution inherited from a past which ignored the vital issues of the Mexican scene and shunned experimentation and the scientific approach. Today, every field of Mexican endeavor is facing reform and more and more faith is being placed in higher learning as the *sine qua non* of national growth and development. Medicine, agriculture, the natural sciences, industry, engineering, these and other bases of modern civilization are taking their place besides the humanities as essential elements in the expression of the best in Mexican culture.

It is not within the scope of this brief study to describe what is being done in these various fields. Each of them warrants special study and comprehensive description and evaluation. The efforts being made to support agricultural education—for children, for peasants, for teachers and for government specialists—by the Federal Government as well as by the states, through departments of education, of agriculture, of Indian affairs, of finance, etc., constitute a remarkable redirection of national interest and of educational policy. Anthropology has become a principal avenue for the study both of Mexico's cultural heritage and the manner in which current action programs can best be adjusted to that heritage. Rural medicine and tropical medicine, fields of vital significance to progress in Mexico, are receiving growing attention in instructional as well as research centers. These activities, though just recently begun, already manifest so many complex aspects that only a detailed individual study of each one could reveal their extent and significance.

Every department of government has suddenly become interested in a scientific approach to the solution of the problems within its jurisdiction. A great variety of centers for technical investigation have been established. Sometimes these centers are associated with some institution of higher learning, but often they exist as independent laboratories or centers of study which serve only indirectly as instructional agencies. The institutions of higher learning, both in Mexico City and elsewhere in the nation, have been encouraging the organization of research and study institutes where the teaching staff is assigned duties for technical investigations of various fields of interest. For example, the National University of Mexico has research institutes in the following fields: mathematics, physics, chemistry, biology, geology, geography, at the National Astronomical Observatory, aesthetic studies, city planning, and other courses in connection with the National Library. Other universities have likewise organized faculty committees and institutes in similar fields. While, as a general rule, these agencies are poorly equipped for research and lack adequate staffs, they nevertheless constitute the springboard from which development in this field of higher studies will, in all probability, rapidly be made within the next few years. The Polytechnic Institute has been giving special attention to research work both by its staff members and by its advanced students. This institution is noteworthy in that research and instruction are much more closely related than is the case in other institutions of higher studies in Mexico. The Instituto de Antropología e Historia, functioning as a semi-autonomous dependency of the Secretariat of Education, has grown to very large proportions in the last few years. It is not only the administering agency for the nation's historic, artistic, and archeological monuments but is also the outstanding center for research and field work in Mexican history and archeology, particularly as they are concerned with the anthropology and ethnology of the native population. It has become a highly important training center as well as the source of numerous fundamental publications. The Secretariat of Education also operates the Instituto de Pedagogía, a research center concerned with the study of the psychological, physiological, social, and economic characteristics of Mexican school children. This institute is doing valuable work in the field of tests and measurements and in the analysis of the factors which should constitute the basis for a scientific program of child welfare.

There are a number of agencies and institutions in Mexico which may be regarded as auxiliary organizations to the program of higher education. The Mexican Commission for Intellectual Cooperation has been established as a semi-autonomous dependency of the Secretariat of Education to promote cooperation in fields of higher education between organizations within the nation and between Mexico and individuals and organizations in other countries. The Pan-American Institute of Geography and History, supported by the governments of the twenty-one American Republics, has its headquarters in Mexico City. This institute has been seeking to sponsor and publish researches in geography and history of particular significance to the Americas and has made solid beginnings as represented by a number of important investigations and publications.

One of the biggest obstacles confronting the development of advanced education and research in Mexico has been the fact that the support and control of higher institutions has fallen to politically constituted departments of government. This, in itself, is not undesirable. However, the failure of the government to safeguard its educational functions from the vicissitudes of factional political strife and of unnecessarily frequent reorganizations has resulted in a serious lack of continuity in educational programs. Furthermore, in the absence of an established educational profession, leadership in educational affairs has come into the hands of scholars and political leaders who have inadequate backgrounds for the exercise of administrative functions in education. Each change of political administration in Mexico has brought about changes in educational programs and policies. Lacinkg professional standards for guidance in educational theory and policy, the destinies of learning have had to respond to the personal views of the individuals whom a political administration has designated as the educational leaders of the moment. Oftentimes this leadership does not survive even through the span of one political administration and educational activities are thus under constant manipulation as a result of the successive changes. The development of higher education in Mexico has been the field of action for personalistic rather than professional leadership. This has been the case to such an extent that this unfortunate characteristic has virtually become a principle in school administration. The heads of universities and other educational institutions and agencies are expected to hold office only for a limited period of time and the "no re-election" policy, eminently desirable in political fields in Mexico, is being accepted as a guiding rule in professional spheres where, obviously, it does not apply. It is a rare educational institution, indeed, that can boast of an administration that has had a tenure lasting as long as four years.

These administrative deficiencies in Mexican higher education are the products of a great variety of antecedents. Barring a concerted attack to remedy them, they can be expected to continue to affect the development of education in Mexico for many years. This is particularly true since the principles of educational administration arise out of governmental practice, it being that qualified independent initiative in educational affairs in Mexico is virtually non-existent.

In this connection, the activities of El Colegio de México are of particular significance. This institution is a politically independent educational foundation which is rendering invaluable service in instructional and research fields. El Colegio de México is not a school. It had its origin in La Casa de España, a privately supported agency established in 1938 to assist Spanish intellectuals, who were refugees from the civil war in Spain, to continue their professional pursuits in Mexico. The private funds of La Casa de España, together with a yearly government grant of 300,000 pesos, became the financial base upon which El Colegio de México was founded as a private institution. This institution is a cooperative undertaking of the Federal Government, the National University, the Bank of Mexico, the Fondo de Cultura Económica (a non-profit publishing firm), and La Casa de España. These cooperative agencies formulate the general policy of El Colegio de México through an Assembly which meets annually. During the course of the year, a small executive committee, together with the Director, acts as the administrative board of the center. The Director, Alfonso Reyes, has had a distinguished career as a diplomat and scholar and is among the world's foremost Spanish-language humanists. Because of its plan of organization, and due to the intelligent leadership of the Director, El Colegio de México has remained free of political pressures and has been able to do independent work in higher education, and follow a planned program consistently and continuously.

El Colegio de México employs both Mexican and foreign scholars to carry out professional studies and researches on a grant-in-aid or fellowship basis. It also employs instructors who are loaned to institutions of higher learning in various parts of the country where they give courses in selected fields of learning. In addition, the Colegio gives financial aid towards the publication of fundamental literary and scientific works. This institution is a bright spot in Mexican higher education. Independent of political administration, it is in a strategic position to exercise leadership in both instructional and research fields. Several of the scholars on the staff are already serving important functions as teachers in the National University and in six institutions of higher learning elsewhere in the nation. Others are busy at work conducting scientific experiments and other researches in a variety of fields. All these activities are carried on without reference to political cross-currents and with only the promotion of professional research, service, and leadership in view. El Colegio de México sponsors the Institute of Physiological Investigations, under the auspices of the Faculty of Medicine of the University of Mexico; the Institute of Chemistry, under the auspices of the School of Chemical Sciences at the Polytechnic Institute; and the Center of Historical Studies, which the Colegio operates independently.

Altruism and philanthropy in the realm of education are not new to

Mexico. From the earliest days of New Spain down to the present there have always been individuals who have used their private wealth to further educational undertakings. Church schools, the public schools of their time, were frequent recipients of such aid. Many of the old colleges were endowed institutions—some individual having given all or a portion of his fortune to the support of a given school. Large bequests of money and other easily convertible valuables were not unusual. The Colegio de Santa María de Todos Santos (see pages 00–00) was a notable product of far-sighted philanthropy. It is interesting to observe the striking similarity between that remarkable institution and El Colegio de México. Three hundred and sixty-seven years after the founding of the Colegio de Santos, there has arisen in Mexico another educational foundation which seeks to enable competent scholars to pursue their studies and public services free from financial limitations and petty obligations. It is to be hoped that this worthy revival of that old-time and intelligent philanthropy may be the beginnings of a new era of private initiative in educational endeavor in Mexico.

As has been implied above, the significance of El Colegio de México transcends the value of its researches or courses. What Mexico, and Latin America generally, are most in need of today in higher education is professional leadership—non-partisan leadership whose tenure is not governed by political alignments, whose goals reach beyond the aim of social or economic vested interests, and whose intellectual equipment enables it to distinguish between issues of transitory import and those which are vital to national growth and development. Intelligent private endeavor everywhere has a decided advantage over public agencies in this regard. In a country like Mexico, where it has become almost axiomatic that educational policy shall respond to the dictates of personal views and politically partisan ends, centers like El Colegio de México have an unusual opportunity to establish norms of scholarship and to maintain professional standards which by their very independence and continuity will serve as guideposts to each succeeding political administration and to every individual who aspires to success in fields of higher learning. This opportunity is a particularly attractive one at this time when Mexico is undergoing a phenomenal educational renaissance and when the Latin American nations are assuming an increasingly important role in hemispheric and world affairs.

The educational centers of Mexico, those which were inherited from the past as well as those of recent creation, reflect a decided growing recognition of the place of science and research in higher learning. Prior to the Revolution, advanced studies followed narrow verbal patterns and little was done to make higher education responsive to the pressing needs of the nation in scientific and technical fields, in the social studies, or in research and administration. Secondary schools were strictly of a college preparatory type—selective, academic, narrowly humanistic. This unresponsiveness of education to Mexican realities was, no doubt, in large measure responsible for the dissatisfaction felt by many intellectuals with the conditions against which the masses revolted at the end of the first decade of the twentieth century. Many of those intellectuals recognized the need of adjusting Mexican life to the demands of a national and a world order in which commerce and industry and their technologies constituted the point of departure for progress. These leaders played no small part in bringing about the Revolution and, after that upheaval, in directing higher education along new paths. The activities carried on today in the centers of higher learning are, in many respects, the carry over of the Revolution into the realm of higher education. Unlike revolutions elsewhere—in France and in Russia, for example—in Mexico the intellectual phase of revolt has followed, and not preceded, the military phase. That intellectual phase is being given overt expression in the reorganization of education along realistic lines. The institutions of higher learning, lagging behind mass education, are just now experiencing the first wave of the revolt.

The new energy with which the Mexican nation is pushing on into the fields of higher learning is most encouraging. From the humble classrooms of village schools to the halls and laboratories of universities, a new spirit permeates the cultural scene. There is a new faith in education, a faith which hopes to find the solution of the nation's vital problems in diligent study and research. That this faith is sometimes incoherent and that it is often inadequately symbolized by the form and practice of educational institutions is not surprising nor disheartening. Mexico's educational renaissance is still in its early stages. Patterns of policy and of procedure are still in the making. Unsatisfactory elements from the heritage of the past still weigh heavily upon popular attitudes and institutional norms. Outmoded structures and practices still persist, often solely for the lack of a workable modern substitute. Yet the curve of education is definitely in a forward and upward direction. Great strides have been taken in mass education. The realism of the primary school has extended rapidly to the upper levels. The secondary schools are becoming popular schools and higher education is no longer a level monopolized by verbalistic studies. This educational change of pace bids well to equip Mexico with the intellectual tools and energy essential to the solving of its pressing social and economic problems and to the assumption of its place among modern nations.

Chapter Five

RESTATEMENT AND CONCLUSION

THIS BRIEF REVIEW of some of the main features of the development of higher education in Mexico will indicate that there are several fundamental trends and issues underlying the intellectual growth of the nation. These trends and issues constitute the basic considerations involved in the crucial problems which confront Mexico in its efforts to achieve a modern program of education. An exhaustive analysis of these questions is not within the scope of this study. However, it would not be complete without at least a rapid review of the major features of Mexican culture which are determining factors in problems confronting Mexican higher education.

Spain left her American colonies a glorious heritage. At its great age in history, it gave generously of the best that European culture had developed up until that time. When the Southern Renaissance was at its best, when Spanish intellectuals were in the vanguard of intellectual endeavor, Spain unstintingly shared its progress with the New World. The full significance of its contributions to culture in Hispanic America can best be appreciated when a careful analysis is made of what Spain was before and during the colonial years and of what it did in sponsoring European culture in America. Don Fernando de los Ríos has made an excellent summary of "Spain in the Epoch of American Colonization" and "The Action of Spain in America" in a recent publication.[1] A study of that summary and of similar analyses by other competent students makes it clear that the cornerstone of Latin American culture represents a great heritage indeed.

The Spanish American scene presents features other than this worthy cultural inheritance, however. Values other than those sponsored by the mother country affected the cultural processes of the New World. The native peoples were an important cultural influence in a great part of Hispanic America. The French *Eclaircissement* gave impetus to ideas which found fertile soil in the Spanish colonies of the Western Hemisphere. Scientific achievements, which had long been on the way and to which Spain had made important contributions, at last found voice in learned circles and a

[1] See: Griffin, *op. cit.,* pp. 25–78.

place in the higher education of Europe, notably in the great universities of Germany; and Latin American institutions could not long remain aloof from these new trends in intellectual activity. The industrial revolution, positivism and materialism, pedagogical developments—these and many other influences were brought to bear upon Spanish America subsequent to Spain's Golden Age. These cultural factors, too, are a phase in the Latin American setting.

The long colonial period, the material obstacles and the physical deficiencies, the complexity of the human factors involved—these and similar circumstances were strong deterrents to intellectual progress in Spanish colonial America. The values inherent in Spain's gifts to her colonies—in art and music, in letters, in administrative techniques, in the *will to do,* in liberal religious fervor—as well as in those gifts which came from other sources, could not achieve their fullest expression in the American environment of the colonial years. Handicapped by the milieu, some of these gifts even degenerated—the *encomienda* system, for example. Others, like the missions, attained only partial success. Still others remained static or made only slow progress. Educational ventures are in this latter category, particularly after the middle of the seventeenth century. The more recent influences found Mexico in political and economic turmoil and their utilization was postponed, awaiting a more propitious occasion.

The chief points in these observations do not depict a situation peculiar to Mexico or to Latin America—they could apply generally in the world wherever an attempt has been made to transplant a culture or to inaugurate new intellectual trends. An appreciation of these facts, however, serves the purpose of aiding in the interpretation of other events in Latin American history. The above circumstances are of particular pertinence in the interpretation of educational developments. The educational patterns implanted by Spain in her American colonies were not far different from, and certainly not inferior to, those then current among other leading nations of the Western World and it is not remarkable that the educational programs of New Spain were characterized by verbalism, by a limited humanism, and by academic formalism: these were the norms of that age in the schools of Europe. It is indeed remarkable that, considering the milieu, these patterns attained such wide acceptance and such conspicuous success in the New World—among Spaniards, *mestizos,* and Indians. What many students criticize is that some major phases of these patterns persisted virtually unchanged even after schools elsewhere had given an important place to newer content, to newer methods, and to newer forms of organiza-tion. But a careful study of the Latin American situation for the period during which these changes were taking place elsewhere will suggest an explanation for such conservatism.

All through the nineteenth century and in the early part of the twentieth, when higher education in northern Europe and in the United States was undergoing a basic remodeling, Latin America was in a politically and economically unsettled state and educational endeavor was at a low ebb. Though the intellectual leaders of the time recognized the values of the new educational trends, they lacked the means to implement the necessary reforms. Their societies, exhausted by the effort expended in obtaining political independence and in carrying out subsequent internal adjustments of the newly won freedoms, were apathetic to the idea of new ventures in education. It is only within very recent years that this situation has changed and, as a result, Latin America is now undergoing an educational awaken-ing.

The experience of Mexico is a good illustration of this lack of social and economic realism with respect to the educational movements of the recent past. In the nineteenth century, for instance, the Royal and Pontifical Uni-versity of Mexico was in no position to open its doors to the newer trends and, therefore, its efforts were limited to trying to live up to the old standards and to the culture represented by its great mother institution—the University of Salamanca. A similar situation obtained in other schools of higher learning in Mexico and in Latin America generally. This inabil-ity to adjust to new currents was in large part misunderstood by the liberal thinkers of the nineteenth century who interpreted such slowness to re-spond to the new methods and content as evidence that the institutions of higher learning were simply instruments of the forces of reaction. Thus the principles of education became political issues, not because the schools were loyal to Spain or because they were dominated by the clergy but because they were loyal to eminently worthwhile intellectual values and did not have the means with which to afford a suitable place in their programs for the new education.

The liberals, out of patience with what they regarded as empty gestures, feared the old intellectual values because of their former sponsorship. They were moved by the new currents of the intellectual world, suppressed the old schools, created a new secondary school, and attacked humanism, theo-retical education, and the like. Later, in 1910, they brought the University back to life with modern and nationalistic goals. But the heritage of a great age was not to be so easily discarded. Almost without knowing it, the higher schools, the preparatory schools as well as the universities, began anew to reach for the old goals and, unconsciously at first, to resist the new tendencies. And so the struggle went on. At times it broke out in factional strife, with the *"universitarios"* becoming politically conservative as they defended humanism and attacked realism, and the supporters of the sciences and technology doing the reverse as they aligned themselves with liberal political groups.

The unfortunate circumstance of Mexico's unpreparedness to revise her educational outlook in the nineteenth century thus converted education into a major political issue. As those who held to the old intellectual values aligned themselves with no faction and as those who saw promise in the newer trends became a part of an opposing group, the educational progress of the nation was left at the mercy of political movements. Liberal governments frowned upon the humanities and theoretical education and smiled on "practical" studies and methods. The National University became a stronghold of traditional intellectual ideas and the Secretariat of Education the champion of technical studies and educational realism. The Instituto Politécnico came into being as a competitor of the University. So, when the friends of the University came into political power, the technical studies at the Instituto were discouraged. When leftists were dominant in the government, the Instituto and its applied sciences were much in vogue and the University was undermined. The intellectual development of the nation, accordingly, has been determined to an important degree by irrelevant considerations which have entered into higher learning and research through the unfortunate association of educational theories and political policies.

The inherent value of the Spanish contribution is undeniable. The intellectual and spiritual values which were planted and cultivated in Mexico stand as monuments to the colonial period and as basic cultural resources of which the nation may well be proud. However, an appreciation of these values and the desire to utilize them fully in the development of a modern Mexican world should not be taken to mean that they suffice. While the traditional intellectual goals of the Royal and Pontifical University of Mexico constitute one of several cultural resources which are highly useful in the forming of a modern program of higher education and while the humanism of the Jesuit schools may with profit be adapted and projected into contemporary institutions, the very appreciation of these values reveals their limitations. Such values, standing alone, are inadequate to meet the realities facing modern Mexico. They represent food for the spirit. But Mexico also has pressing physical needs. It needs science, it needs techniques of administration. It needs those intellectual contributions which, though they have entered the cultural scene only recently, are indispensable attributes of higher learning in the modern world. On the other hand, the value of and need for the sciences does not deny the worth of the traditional values.

The cultural issue facing Mexico and Latin America is not that of choosing between the humanities and the sciences. These ways of thought and schemes of values are not alternatives nor are they mutually exclusive. They are correlative and the Latin Americas need both of them. With due appreciation for the great contributions made in classical education during colonial times, it would be folly to ignore the limitations of the colonial heritage and it would be disastrous to fail to recognize the inadequacy of seventeenth-century methods in a twentieth-century society. That, however, does not imply that these traditional means and values have no place in the modern social structure. On the other hand, the fact that scientific content and methods did not form an important part of the colonial heritage in no way denies their value in the development of a well-balanced culture, in Mexico or elsewhere in Latin America.

The struggle between the old patterns of intellectual endeavor and the new fields of learning referred to above has constituted the dominant issue in Mexican higher education for many years. Failure to arrive at a working agreement with reference to this issue and the uncertainty as to what should be the content and methods of higher education have constituted the chief stumbling block in the way of the proper development of the administrative techniques and structures and those professional standards which are essential to the satisfactory operation and growth of a modern Mexican society. This uncertainty expresses itself, for example, in the fear to entrust the administration of educational institutions, for long, to any one person, board, or council. In a desire to safeguard the National University against the inroads of political administrations regarded by some as too liberal, Mexico has gone to the extreme of virtually forestalling the establishment of professional standards and has handicapped the continuity of institutional policies and the very security of university life.[2] That same fear has caused

---

[2] See the *Anuarios* of the University of Mexico for the regulations which cover these phases of typical university organization.

institutions of higher learning to give to student bodies an equal voice with their professors in the administration of the schools, in the formulation of their curricula, and in controlling vital phases of teaching and scholarship. With all due regard to the advantages of student participation in school government, it is clear that there are professional phases of higher education which are not within the competence of the students. Autonomy in higher education has been jeopardized by placing the institutions too much at the mercy of the students. In seeking to avoid dominance by vested interests within the political sphere, the universities have laid themselves open to political manipulation by students and by those who can incite students. It is doubtful whether academic freedom or professional norms have been the gainer by this sort of "autonomy."

The problems which arise in the case of these aspects of higher education in Mexico would be found to appear anew in connection with other features of higher learning and research. It is not the purpose of this treatise to analyze these weaknesses. But it is the intention here to indicate that, in Mexico's struggle to make the transition from the intellectual world of the colony to one consonant with the requirements of a modern age, irrelevant issues and questionable practices have got into the Mexican educational picture. How to correct these weaknesses constitutes one of the most pressing challenges facing Mexican educational reformers. If approached with the proper perspective, it will be apparent that the remedial action required is neither a denial of Mexico's cultural heritage nor an attempt to inject some foreign "ism" into Mexican policy. The autonomy of Mexico's universities must be implemented with the procedures and mechanisms which will make that autonomy effective and real, and which will safeguard it against those who would destroy it either from within or from without.

The educational leadership of the nation must be prepared to distinguish between relevant and irrelevant issues in Mexican educational growth. The political principle of "effective suffrage—no re-election" is of doubtful validity in the administration of institutions of learning. The same is true of the Church question for, in the last analysis, Mexico can be a Catholic country and still be a modern, progressive, and intelligent country. Catholicism does not imply intellectual stagnation or indifference to human welfare and progress. That is to say, sound school administration and intelligent educational development is not incompatible with the proper observance of religious beliefs. Education need have no quarrel with the Church in Mexico and, by the same token, the Church need have no quarrel with modern education. The political aspect of the Church-State question is no more relevant to the basic interests of centers of higher learning and research than is any other political issue. And so on for many other live issues in Mexican education.

The Mexican intellectual heritage, like that of virtually all of Latin America, is a varied and a highly attractive one. Its variety is an asset of undeniable worth in cultural development. But aside from its variety, it is a field presenting a peculiar situation and one of great intellectual promise. There, the values inherent in humanism in a classical-theoretical education are still contemporary values. Whereas in countries such as the United States these values have lost much ground to technology and are more remote in educational history, in Mexico they still have an important hold upon the curricula of secondary and higher schools. In addition, Mexico's educational institutions are rapidly making room for those newer fields of learning in which the schools of her northern neighbor have excelled. With care, these new technical and scientific contributions can become a part of Mexican higher education without impairing, but rather as properly balancing the older, more broadly cultural values. The attainment of such a balance in higher education is a very worthwhile goal. Important steps have already been taken in this direction by Mexican institutions. The success thus far attained and the promise of larger returns as these gains are expanded constitute a stirring challenge to Mexican intellectuals.

BIBLIOGRAPHY

Aguayo Spencer, Rafael (Ed.). *Don Vasco De Quiroga*. Mexico, Editorial Polis, 1940. 472 pp.

Alegría, Paula. *La Educación En México Antes Y Después De La Conquista*. Mexico, Editorial "Cultura," 1936. 284 pp.

Avila Camacho, Manuel. "México Debe Ser País Agricola E Industrial," Secretaría de Gobernación, Mexico, 1941. 15 pp.

Bach, Federico. *Mexico Today, The Annals* of The American Academy of Political and Social Science, Volume 208, March 1940. pp. 70–77.

Basauri, Carlos. *La Población Indígena De México*. Mexico, Secretaría de Educación Pública, Oficina Editora Popular, 1940. Volumes I, II. 363 pp., 568 pp.

Blair, Evelyn. "Educational Movements In Mexico, 1821–1836," unpublished doctoral dissertation, The University of Texas, 1941.

Bonavit, Julián. *Historia del Colegio Primitivo y Nacional de San Nicolás de Hidalgo*. Morelia, Departamento de Extensión Universitaria, 1940. 341 pp.

Castañeda, C. E. "Beginnings of Printing in America," *Preliminary Studies of the Texas Catholic Historical Society,* Volume III, Number 7, November, 1940 (reprint from The American Historical Review, Volume XX, Number 4, November, 1940). 19 pp.

―――― *Nuevos Documentos Inéditos O Muy Raros Para La Historia De México*. Mexico, Talleres Gráficos de la Nación, 1939. 216 pp.

―――― "The Beginnings of University Life in America," *Preliminary Studies of the Texas Catholic Historical Association,* Volume III, No. 4, July, 1938.

―――― "The First American Play," *Preliminary Studies of the Texas Catholic Historical Society,* Volume III, Number I, Janury 1, 1936. 39 pp.

―――― "The First Printing Press in Mexico," *The Publishers' Weekly.* January 6, 1940. pp. 50–53.

―――― "These Things Began in Mexico," *Today and Tomorrow* (discontinued), March 1, 1941. pp. 28–29.

Chávez, Ezequiel A. *El Primero de los Grandes Educadores de la América, Fray Pedro de Gante*. Mexico, Imprenta Mundial, 1934. 106 pp.

Covarrubias, José Díaz. *La Instrucción Pública en México*. Mexico, Imprenta, de Gobierno, 1875.

Decorme, S. J., Gerard. *La Obra de los Jesuitas Mexicanos Durante la Epoca Colonial 1572–1767*. Mexico. Antigua Libreria Robredo de José Porrúa e Hijos. 1941. Volumes I and II. 518 pp., 635 pp.

Gamio, Manuel, "Geographic and Social Handicaps," *Mexico Today, The Annals* of the American Academy of Political and Social Science, Volume 208, March, 1940. pp. 1–11.

Griffin, Charles C. (Ed.). *Concerning Latin American Culture*. New York, Columbia University Press (For the National Committee of the United States of America on Intellectual Cooperation), 1940. 234 pp.

Gruening, Ernest. *Mexico and Its Heritage*, New York, D. Appleton-Century Company, 1934. 728 pp.

Jones, Chester Lloyd. "Production of Wealth in Mexico," *Mexico Today, The Annals* of the American Academy of Political and Social Science, Volume 208, March 1940. pp. 55–69.

Macías, Pablo G. *Aula Nobilis*, Morelia, Michoacán, Mexico. Monografía del Colegio Primitivo y Nacional de San Nicolás de Hidalgo. 1940. 620 pp.

Mendizábal, Miguel O. de. *Ensayos Sobre Las Civilizaciones Aborígenes Americanas*. Mexico, Museo Nacional, 1924. Vol. I. 347 pp.

Molina Enríquez, Andrés. *La Revolución Agraria De México*, Mexico, Museo Nacional de Arqueología Historia y Etnografía, 1932. (Four volumes). Vol. I. 158 pp.

Novedades (newspaper), November 18, 1941.

Palacios, Juan Enrique. "El Calendario y Jeroglíficos Cronográficos Mayas," *Primer Centenario de la Sociedad Mexicana de Geografía y Estadística*, Mexico, 1933. Volume II, pp. 457–635.

Priestley, Herbert. *The Mexican Nation*. New York, The Macmillan Company, 1930. 507 pp.

Redfield, Robert. *Mexico Today, The Annals* of the American Academy of Political and Social Science, Volume 208, March 1940. pp. 132–143.

Reyes, Alfonso. *Pasado Inmediato Y Otros Ensayos*. Mexico, El Colegio de México, 1941. 194 pp.

Romero Flores, Jesús. *Anales Históricos De La Revolución Mexicana*. Biblioteca Del Maestro. Mexico, El Nacional, 1939. (Volumes I, II, III, IV.) Volume I. 274 pp.

Romero Flores, Jesús *et al. IV Centenario de Morelia, 1541–1941*. Commemorative monograph (publisher unknown). 123 pp.

Sánchez, Geo. I. "Education," *Mexico Today, The Annals* of the American Academy of Political and Social Science, Volume 208, March, 1940. pp. 144–152.

—— "Educational Crisis in Mexico," *Butrava*, Annual Bulletin of The Bureau of University Travel, No. 6, February, 1942. pp. 4–7.

—— "Group Differences and Spanish-Speaking Children—A Critical Review." *Journal of Applied Psychology,* Volume XVI, No. 5, October 1932. pp. 549–558.

—— *Mexico—A Revolution by Education.* New York, the Viking Press, 1936. 211 pp.

Sánchez Mejorada, Javier. *Mexico Today, The Annals* of the American Academy of Political and Social Science, Volume 208, March 1940. pp. 78–93.

Secretaría de Educación Nacional, Departamento de Enseñanza Técnica, "Planes de Estudios De Las Carreras Que Se Cursan En El Instituto Politécnico Nacional 1940," (mimeographed bulletin).

Instituto Politécnico Nacional, Anuario, Mexico, 1939. 89 pp.

Secretaría de Educación Pública. *Memoria, 1940–1941.* Mexico, 1941.

Secretaría de Gobernación, Departamento de Plan Sexenal. *Seis Años de Gobierno al Servicio de México,* 1934–1940. Mexico, La Nacional Impresora, S.A., 1940, 459 pp.

Secretaría de la Economía Nacional,

La Reforma Agraria En México, Dirección General de Estadística, 1937. (Twenty colored charts with accompanying statistical analyses.)

México En Cifras, Dirección General de Estadística, 1934 and 1938. (Statistical atlases.)

Teja Zabre, Alfonso. *Guide to the History of Mexico.* Mexico, Press of the Ministry of Foreign Affairs, 1935. 375 pp.

Universidad Michoacana de San Nicolás de Hidalgo,

Anales del Museo Michoacano, Morelia, No. 1, July 1939. pp. 42–57.

Universidad Michoacana, Bulletin of the University of Michoacán, Morelia, July 1939. pp. 3–27.

Hacia La Reforma Universitaria. Publication of the University of Michoacán, Morelia, 1939. 84 pp.

Universidad Nacional Autónoma De México. *Anuario.* (One issued for each school or faculty.)

Watson, Goodwin. "Education and Social Welfare in Mexico." A report, The Council for Pan American Democracy, January, 1940. 47 pp.

Wilson, Irma. *Mexico, a Century of Educational Thought.* New York, Hispanic Institute in the United States, 1941. 376 pp.

Zepeda Rincón, Tomás. *La Instrucción Pública En La Nueva España En El Siglo XVI.* Mexico, Universidad Nacional de México, 1933. 138 pp.

Zollinger, Edwin. *Enrique C. Rébsamen.* Translated from the German by Soloman Kahan. Mexico, Secretaría de Educación Pública, 1935. 100 pp.

INDEX